D0940502

IN THE NEAR LOSS OF
EVERYTHING

George MacDonald's Son
in America

DALE WAYNE SLUSSER

"Readers of George MacDonald's writings and life will especially enjoy Dale Wayne Slusser's informative and untold story of MacDonald's son, Ronald, during his struggling life in America. *In the Near Loss of Everything* reveals that Ronald MacDonald – headmaster, novelist, fairytale writer, and playwright – inherited more than his father's literary talent; like his father, he also personified the role of Greatheart throughout his life."

Glenn Edward Sadler, editor of
An Expression of Character: The Letters of George MacDonald

"Dale Wayne Slusser's careful research of primary documents is artfully presented in this absorbing account of the life of George MacDonald's son, Ronald. His father's influence is clearly evident in Ronald's comments about life, death, and the Christian life. *In the Near Loss of Everything* also provides readers with a unique glimpse into the lives of Ronald's parents and siblings."

David L. Neuhouser, Scholar in Residence, Taylor University
Center for the Study of C. S. Lewis and Friends

"Dale Slusser's book would be a special treat for George MacDonald enthusiasts, if only for its appendices. In them we get fascinating, out of print samples of Ronald MacDonald's own writing: parts of a fairy tale, and Ronald's remembrances of his father and comments on his father's work. But Slusser does much more. In this account of Ronald's time in America, and the troubles he shared there with his wife and sister, Slusser adds an important missing piece to our knowledge of the MacDonald family and its stuggles. And in telling the story of a man who did not give up, Slusser allows Ronald to do what his father has so often done: inspire and encourage. Well researched and well worth the having."

Jeff McInnis, author of
Shadows and Chivalry: C.S. Lewis and George MacDonald on Suffering, Evil, and Goodness.

IN THE NEAR LOSS OF EVERYTHING
Copyright © 2009 Dale Wayne Slusser
Allentown, PA

All rights reserved. Except in the case of quotations embodied in
critical articles or reviews, no part of this book may be reproduced or
transmitted in any form or by any means, electronic or mechanical,
including photocopying, recording, or by any information storage or
retrieval system, without written permission of the publisher.
For information, contact Zossima Press www.Zossima.com

Zossima Press titles may be purchased for business or promotional use or special sales.

10-9-8-7-6-5-4-3-2-1

ISBN   0-9822385-3-3
ISBN 13   978-0-9822385-3-0

"In such an hour, a man's heart, be he the sick or the whole, will tell him: "This is the time for saying and hearing all that has never yet been heard nor said between us. This is the moment when passion may distil its finest essence. In the near loss of everything but our spiritual relation we may know, perhaps, and touch each other with an intimacy never yet attained — reaching, for a moment before the last curtain falls between, almost to the secret of that eternal relation which underlies the mystery of man and woman."

Ronald MacDonald, *The Carcase* (1909)

TABLE OF CONTENTS

SELECT LIST OF ILLUSTRATIONS

ACKNOWLEDGEMENTS

This book has been 15 years in the making, and was slow going at the start. Being what's now referred to as a "digital alien," much of my early research was done via correspondence through the postal services or through visits to local institutions. Later as I became more computer literate I was able to make contacts, order materials and search databases through the use of e-mail and the internet.

My first contact and real start of the project was through the Old Buncombe County Genealogical Society, in their humble quarters here in Asheville. It was there that I first found the reference to Louise MacDonald's death and burial in a book of records from Trinity Episcopal Church.

Speaking of Trinity Episcopal Church, I must acknowledge the help of Mary Parker. Mary, a parishioner of Trinity, is a noted historian of the church as well as a retired member of our local Library system. But even more importantly to our story, she is the daughter of Haywood Parker, the headmaster at Ravenscroft who Ronald MacDonald came to replace in 1889. Miss Parker's father Haywood, and Ronald and Louise were also fellow parishioners at Trinity. Mary's maternal grandfather, Col. Thomas Patton (whose house Mary now lives in) was a member of the Board of Fellows of Ravenscroft, and is mentioned in our story.

Special thanks to Barbara Amell, editor of the *Wingfold* quarterly periodical, for publishing my original article in 1995, and for her references to material on Ronald MacDonald. And I also thank Larry E. Fink for use of the Casa Coraggio photographs.

At the start of my research I was aided by John Docherty, then Honorable Secretary of the George MacDonald Society in England.

From the early days of plowing through the shelf-long volumes of the *Dictionary of British and American Authors* and searching the vertical files, to last years' hours of usage of the microfilm readers, the staff of the Pack Memorial Library of the Buncombe County Public Libraries have been of invaluable assistance to me. Specifically I acknowledge the staff of the North Carolina Collections for their friendly and diligent help: Ann S. Wright and Zoe Rhine.

The Beinecke Library at Yale and its staff have been very helpful to my research. Being the main repository for the George MacDonald family letters, the bulk of material for this story came from the letters in their George MacDonald Collection. Former director Vincent Giroud was invaluable as his extensive knowledge of the collection first let me know how many letters were from Ronald and Lilia in the collection. This was useful years later as it helped focus my ordering of microfilm copies of the letters. Karen Nangle graciously handled all my inquiries and numerous e-mails and microfilm orders.

Thanks also to the Museum of the Confederacy in Richmond, Virginia for making their inventory of their Jefferson Davis Family Collection available on-line. It was from that inventory that I found the letter from Alfred Blandy to Jefferson Davis, which confirmed their connection. My research of the MacDonald's time at Pottstown was greatly aided by the assistance of Willis Pierre, retired teacher from Hill School. Thanks also to Jenny Neophytou of London who was instrumental in obtaining a copy of *The Green Handkerchief.*

Several British institutions should be acknowledged for their aid in research and their permission to publish their material. The Ruskin Library at the University of Lancaster was very helpful in my research of Louise Blandy and her relationship to John Ruskin. Not only did they send me the requested copies of letters, but they accepted my suggestion and took on the arduous task of scanning Louise's scrapbooks in their collection. The quality of the scans was impeccable. Thank you especially to Diane Tyler for her many e-mails and handling of my requests. The Ruskin Collection of the Sheffield Galleries & Museums Trust, specifically Louise Pullen, is to be thanked for the scans of Louise's drawings from their collection.

For editorial assistance I must first thank my dear wife for reading of all my drafts, as well as for her sacrificing many Saturdays and evenings to my research. Thanks are in order also to my friend, Joe Franklin, who not only provided insight on the initial drafts of the manuscript, but whose enthusiasm for the project has been an impetus in my pursuing publishing. Many thanks to Dr. Don King of Montreat College in Black Mountain, NC for his academic editing of my manuscripts, as well as his advice and encouragement throughout the project. Retired Professor, Dr. Glenn Edward Sadler, MacDonald author and aficionado, whom I first met in 1995, has not only advised me on my manuscript, but has been an encouragement through the many years of my research.

Finally, I acknowledge that there are still many unanswered questions about Ronald & Louise and their experiences in America. Therefore I appeal to you reader – if you have any additional information about Ronald MacDonald and/or his wife Louise Blandy MacDonald, or any of their descendents, or find any additional references to them and their relationships to Ravenscroft High School or Hill School, please contact me at: dws@helps1228.org or the publisher at: Robert@ Zossima.com.

Preface

I read: "He and his wife went out to Asheville in North Carolina where Ronald became headmaster at an Episcopal school named Ravenscroft." I was intrigued. Not only was I an avid fan of Ronald's father, author George MacDonald, whose biography I was reading, but I had also just moved to Asheville! Then a few sentences later I read, "Ronald's school was not a notable success, and to add to his difficult lot, his wife died in 1890." I was hooked! Knowing that Ronald was still in Asheville in 1890, I assumed, and rightly so, that his wife, Louise Virenda Blandy MacDonald, had died here and likely was buried here as well. Thus began a decade and a half of research to uncover this sad, but intriguing story.

This story is one in which many people can identify. First, on an emotional level, anyone who has ever been newly married, or suffered with profound homesickness, or depression, or has experienced extreme grief due to the loss of a beloved spouse will feel empathy toward Ronald and Louise and the entire MacDonald family.

Second, those interested in historical and sociological issues will find many interesting facts and events, many heretofore unpublished, surrounding the histories of Ravenscroft School, the City of Asheville and The Hill School in Pottstown, Pennsylvania. The contemporary descriptions of life, through the letters of those who were living at the time, give us a better "feel" for the life of these towns and institutions, than mere rote descriptions in "history books" can give.

Third, die-hard George MacDonald fans will find material that will enhance their understanding of the beloved author, whose writings were very much a product of the myriad of divine crucibles which touched his family and life. During the period covered in this story (1889-94), when Ronald was just beginning his career, George MacDonald was at the end of his many years of writing, and his last work, *Lilith,* was finished the next year, 1895. George empathized with Ronald's loss and felt deeply for his dear son who was alone in a foreign country, far from the consolation of his family. Not only did George empathize with Ronald's loss, but he himself would again go through another crucible soon after Ronald's, with the death of his beloved daughter Lilia.

After giving us a long list of people who by faith suffered and died, the author of the book of Hebrews, in the Bible, encourages his audience: *"Therefore since we are surrounded by such a cloud of witnesses, let us throw off everything that hinders…"* In the same way, I hope this story will encourage readers that we are not alone in our sufferings – many before us have experienced the same kinds of trials and testing as we have (that cloud of witnesses). In this story we will see how one man experienced tragedy and loss, and yet persevered through it and afterward went on to live a fruitful and productive life.

Dale Wayne Slusser
"Daelscroft"
Asheville, North Carolina

8

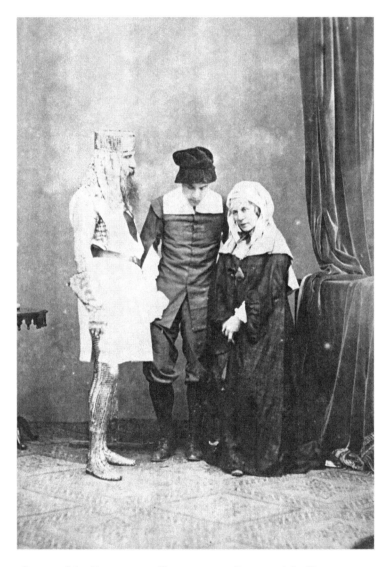

George MacDonald as Greatheart, Ronald MacDonald as Feeble-Mind, and Louisa MacDonald as Mistress Muchafraid in the family production of *Pilgrim's Progress II* circa 1877.

CHAPTER I

RONALD & LOUISE

Surrounding every famous man or woman of history are myriads of unfamed family and friends who have their own personal stories, often overlooked or hidden in the shadows of the famous. One such story is that of Ronald MacDonald, son of George MacDonald, famed Victorian author. The story of Ronald's seven year sojourn in America (1887-1894) and the tragic loss of his wife, Louise Virenda, is the focus of our story. The story will be told from material gleaned mostly from the MacDonald family letters (many of them unpublished) along with other documents and records of the period.

Ronald MacDonald was born on October 27, 1860, to George and Louisa MacDonald, the seventh of eleven children. George MacDonald, who had just published his first book, *Phantastes*, two years earlier (1858), would become a noted author, poet and preacher, and by the end of the nineteenth century brought himself and his large family both notoriety and fame. Although George MacDonald published about 50 works in his lifetime, much of it was before adequate copyright laws were established, so the family never achieved any financial security in his lifetime. Though they were never rich, nor of the titled gentry, MacDonald's writing and popularity put them into such social circles that they were intimate friends with many notable Victorians, including, John Ruskin, Lord & Lady Mount-Temple, Lady Byron, Lewis Carroll, Kate Terry, Sir Edward & Georgiana Burne-Jones, Arthur Hughes, Edward Hughes, Alexander Munro, and Sir John & Lady Effie Millais. These social connections and exposure to the arts played a role in the lives of the MacDonald children. Ronald not only married an artist, but himself became a novelist and playwright.

The entire family had an interest in the theatre arts. In 1876, Louisa MacDonald formed a family theatrical troupe which toured the country for "charity"– that is, their *own* charity – to supplement the family's often meager income. The family productions had a long two decade run, giving performances even after all the children had reached adulthood. Ronald acted in the troupe, taking various roles. In the family's popular production of "Pilgrims Progress"[1] he played the part of "Greatheart" when his father was unavailable to take the part. His father, while on a lecture tour in England in 1889, writes to his mother, while staying with a hosting family, that he received a request for a performance of "Pilgrim's Progress." He writes: "Perhaps it may be possible, especially if Ronald comes home again."[2]

On July 14, 1883, *The Era*, a London newspaper, reported that the MacDonald family performed a costume recital of an adaptation of Corneille's "Polyeuctus" at Steinway Hall, with Ronald taking the role of Severus.

Prior to his sojourn in America, Ronald obtained his BA in history, from Trinity College, Oxford in 1885. Almost immediately upon receiving his degree, he took a position as a master (teacher) at Clifton Boy's School in Bristol. The next year he left Clifton for a new position at Cathedral School in Gloucester. It was during these years that he met and fell in love with a young artist, Louise Virenda Blandy. Louise Virenda, third of six children, was born to Alfred and Ozillah Harris Blandy in 1861. Louise or Virenda (she alternately went by either name) was born in Baltimore, Maryland, where her father, Dr. Alfred Addison Blandy, held the position of Professor of Dental Surgery at the Baltimore College of Dental Surgery. The College was co-founded in 1840 by Blandy's father-in-law, Chapin A. Harris. Dr. Blandy, born in Bristol, England in 1824, moved to America at the age of eight with his parents and numerous siblings. Raised in Zanesville, Ohio, by 1850 he had married Ozillah and was living in Baltimore and active as a professor, dental surgeon and editor of numerous dental magazines. Dr. Blandy

---

1   Hein, Rolland. *George MacDonald: Victorian Mythmaker*, Nashville: Star Song Publishing,1993), pp. 287-88.

2   Letter from George MacDonald to Louisa MacDonald dated October 1, 1889 – George MacDonald Collection. General Collection, Beinecke Rare Book and Manuscript Library, Yale University.

was advancing quickly in this new professional field of dental surgery, and in 1858 he even patented a new alloy of tin, called "cheoplasty" for use in making dentures. All of that changed dramatically with the advent of the Civil War. In 1864, Dr. Blandy found himself facing prosecution on a swindling charge that, combined with Union hostility towards him for being a "blatant secessionist," caused him to flee the United States for Brazil. It is reported that soon after moving to Brazil he acquired the position of Acting British Consul at Belem, Brazil.[3] Reversing the steps of his father, Alfred Blandy moved his family to England sometime around 1868, and set up a dental surgery practice in the prestigious Harley Street in London. Dr. Blandy maintained his confederate ties, even after moving back to England[4].

Louise, not being yet seven years old when they moved to England, probably did not remember much about living in the United States. And, owing to the fact that a number of confederate ex-patriots had already established themselves in London, the family soon became immersed in British society and culture. One of those ex-pats was Louise's aunt Sadie (Zairah Harris Mignot) and her artist husband Louis Rémy Mignot[5], who fled the U.S. at the start of the Civil War and moved to London in 1862. The Mignots were heavily involved in the art society of London and by 1863 Mignot was exhibiting his work in the Royal Academy beside the work of established British artists.[6]

3   Hanna, Alfred Jackson and Hanna, Kathryn Abbey. *Confederate Exiles in Venezuela*. (Tuscaloosa, Alabama: Confederate Publishing Company, Inc 1960), p. 25.: See also, report of James B. Bond, US Consul at Para, Brazil to US Secretary of State, Washington, DC- October 15, 1864. – U. S. National Archives, Group 59 Roll 2.

4   In 1868 he is noted as one the officers of "The Chartered American, English and Venezuelan Trading and Commercial Company". The business of the company was to promote emigration, both from North America and Europe, to a 240,000 square mile land grant in Venezuela. The purpose of the grant was "to provide a home for those in the south, who… could not remain in their old homes under the vulgar domination of their heartless victors: and for the poor confederate soldiers and their widows and orphans". See- http://books.google.com/books?id=nR kIAAAAQAAJ&pg=PA111&dq=vade+mecum+Venezuela#PPA88,M1.

5   Louis Rémy Mignot (b. 1831, Charleston, SC – d. 1870, London) – Unfortunately, only eight years later in 1870, Mignot contracted small pox and died. Although he was not alive when Louise began her art lessons with Ruskin, certainly he had some influence on her considering such a career. Mignot's acquaintance with Ruskin would likely have been predisposed Ruskin to accepting Louise as a pupil.

6   Manthorne, Katherine E. and Coffey, John. *The Landscapes of Louis Rémy Mignot: A Southern Painter Abroad*. (Raliegh, NC: North Carolina Museum of Art, 1996) – See Chapter 7 – "The Confederate Painter in Victorian Britain".

The Blandy family became part of that Victorian British art world, if for no other reason, on account of their association with the Mignots. Louise must have exhibited promising artistic talent at a young age, for by 1873, at the age of 12 or 13, she began corresponding with noted artist, author and art critic, John Ruskin. Ruskin wrote to Louise on March 18, 1873: "I did not get the pretty photograph till yesterday on arriving from Oxford- I like it very much, it is like you[…]. You are a dear little lady for sending it (to) me with your love."[7] By 1874 she had begun taking art lessons from Ruskin. Her talent blossomed and in 1879 she was invited by Sir Coutts Lindsay to exhibit a painting of "Vase & Flowers" in the Water Colour Hall of his recently built Grosvenor Gallery. Her painting soon sold for £5.5.[8] It was a thrill for Louise, at the age of 18, to have her painting hanging in the same exhibition with such famous exhibitors as Sir Lawrence Alma-Tadema, Sir Edward Burne-Jones, Edward R. Hughes,[9] Sir John Millais, Sir Edward Poynter and even HRH Princess Louise (daughter of Edward VII).[10] Louise was again invited in 1880 to "contribute to the Water Colour Section of the coming Winter Exhibition."[11] She did not contribute to that exhibition but instead soon entered a painting titled "Water Lilies" in an exhibition at the Walker Art Gallery in Liverpool, which sold for £6.07.[12]

In the years following her exhibitions, and on into the 1880s, Louise continued her artistic endeavors. She remained in contact with Ruskin during those years and often undertook copying for him. Two of her works, a drawing of a staircase in Bargello, near Florence and a copy of seven of the angels from Fra Angelico's 'Resurrection' in the National Gallery were placed in the collection of the Museum of

---

7   Louise Blandy Scrapbook-RF B 9, Ruskin Foundation (Ruskin Library, Lancaster University)

8   Louise Blandy Scrapbook-RF 1996B2838, Ruskin Foundation (Ruskin Library, Lancaster University)

9   Edward Hughes was engaged to Ronald's sister Mary, but Mary died in 1878, before they could marry.

10   See list of 1879 Exhibitors – Christopher Newall, *The Grosvenor Gallery Exhibitions: Change and continuity in the Victorian art world*. (Cambridge: Cambridge University Press, 1995), pp. 143-145.

11   Louise Blandy Scrapbook-RF 1996B2838, Ruskin Foundation (Ruskin Library, Lancaster University)

12   Louise Blandy Scrapbook-RF 1996B2838, Ruskin Foundation (Ruskin Library, Lancaster University)

the Guild of St. George, Sheffield."[13] Though many of Louise's works have been lost or at least undiscovered, enough remains as evidence to her consummate artistic talent. Her ability as an artist, especially her proficiency in pencil and chalk, are shown by the sketches to be found in her scrapbooks[14], as well as from her portrait of the singer Antoinette Stirling Mackinlay[15] which now hangs in the National Portrait Gallery in England.

ANTOINETTE STIRLING MACKINLAY
DRAWING BY LOUISE VIRENDA BLANDY

It is not clear how or where Ronald and Louise first met. However, it is easy to see that they had numerous mutual connections whereby

13   Robert Hewison, *Ruskin and Oxford: The Art of Education.* (Oxford: Clarendon Press, 1996), p.72.

14   Louise Blandy Scrapbook-RF 1996B2838, Ruskin Foundation (Ruskin Library, Lancaster University)

15   NPG 2774 – Antoinette Mackinlay (née Stirling) by Louise Virenda Blandy – chalk, 1880. Primary Collection. National Portrait Gallery, England. The George MacDonalds were friends of the MacKinlays- see letter from George MacDonald to John & Antoinette MacKinlay, October 6, 1887. – Glenn Edward Sadler, *An Expression of Character: The Letters of George MacDonald.* (Grand Rapids, MI: Wm. B Eerdmmans Publishing, 1994), pp. 326-28.

they could have met. We know that Louise's father was Ruskin's dentist and that Ruskin was also a friend of the MacDonald family. Also the MacDonalds were intimates with many of the British artists of their day, in which circles Louise was no doubt a part. They met and were dating by the fall of 1886. Ronald's sister Irene writes from England to their mother in Italy, on September 19, 1886: "Ronald and Virenda came in and carried us off to town."[16] They soon fell in love, evidenced by Louise's short notation handwritten on the top a playbill (in one of her scrapbooks) for the Royal Court Theatre performance of "Dandy Dick." The note reads: "January 31, 1887- (R & L <u>alone</u>)."[17] They became engaged to be married in April of 1887.

SKETCHES BY LOUISE BLANDY

UNKNOWN BABY (OZELLA?)
– FROM LOUISE'S SCRAPBOOK-
RF 1996B2838, RUSKIN FOUNDATION
(RUSKIN LIBRARY, LANCASTER UNIVERSITY)

UNKNOWN GIRL- FROM LOUISE'S SCRAPBOOK
RF 1996B2838, RUSKIN FOUNDATION
(RUSKIN LIBRARY, LANCASTER UNIVERSITY)

---

16   Letter from Irene MacDonald to Louisa MacDonald dated September 19, 1886 – George MacDonald Collection. General Collection, Beinecke Rare Book and Manuscript Library, Yale University.

17   Louise Blandy Scrapbook-RF 1996B2838, Ruskin Foundation (Ruskin Library, Lancaster University)

B.P.MD. R.7.MD. G.MM D. G.MD. R.MD. M.MD. G.MK.MD,

Porto Fino

GEORGE MACDONALD (CENTER) AND HIS SONS. PORTO FINO, ITALY, 1878.
FROM LEFT TO RIGHT: BERNARD, ROBERT, GREVILLE,
GEORGE, RONALD, MAURICE, AND MACKAY
COURTESY BEINECKE LIBRARY, YALE UNIVERSITY

PORTOFINO IS A SMALL ITALIAN FISHING VILLAGE AND TOURIST RESORT ON THE ITALIAN RIVIERA.
THE TOWN CROWDED ROUND ITS SMALL HARBOUR IS CONSIDERED TO BE AMONG THE MOST
BEAUTIFUL MEDITERRANEAN PORTS.

Casa Coraggio

IN QUESTA "CASA CORAGGIO"
TRA IL 1879 ED IL 1902
VISSE ED OPERO'
LO SCRITTORE SCOZZESE

GEORGE MAC DONALD

1824 — 1905

IL COMUNE DI BORDIGHERA 18.09.1986

CASA CORAGGIO IN BORDIGHERA, ITALY
PHOTOS COURTESY OF LARRY E. FINK

❖ CHAPTER 2 ❖

BOUND FOR AMERICA

George MacDonald's biographers all say that Ronald left to move to America with his bride in 1889. However, the MacDonald family letters reveal a different story. Ronald first sailed to America as a single man (though engaged) in the summer of 1887, leaving Louise behind in England, under the watchful care of the MacDonald family. At this time the MacDonald family was living most of the year at their home in Bordighera, Italy, returning to England for the summers. The large stone house, named Casa Coraggio, was built for the family through the generosity of their friends for the sake of the MacDonald family's propensity for lung and tuberculin ailments. Also, by this time, three of the boys, Bob, Bernard and MacKay were in College or training in England. In fact, in August 1886, George MacDonald writes to his son Bob, from Casa Coraggio – "…We have no boys with us at present; perhaps we may never all meet together again in this world. God knows…."[18] In addition, Greville, the oldest boy, was beginning his practice as a physician in Harley Street. Ronald's sister Winifred writes to Ronald from Greville's new house and clinic where the younger family members had gathered to help Greville clean and set up: "Louise & Maud [Louise's sister] came over to help us with the house yesterday, & if the amount of work done could be estimated by the blackness of our hands, we did an immense quantity."[19]

---

18   Letter from George MacDonald to Robert Falconer MacDonald, August 29, 1886. – Glenn Edward Sadler, *An Expression of Character: The Letters of George MacDonald*. (Grand Rapids, MI: Wm. B Eerdmmans Publishing, 1994), pp. 320.

19   Letter from Winifred MacDonald to Ronald MacDonald dated June 21, 1887 – George MacDonald Collection. General Collection, Beinecke Rare Book and Manuscript Library, Yale University.

Ronald's ultimate destination was Hill School in Pottstown, Pennsylvania, where he had taken a position as one of the masters (teachers). But, he first had accepted a private tutoring position for the summer. He writes on September 13, 1887, to his mother on stationery from The Malvern, a hotel in Bar Harbor Maine:

> Dearest Mammy,
>
> I got your dear letter dated Aug. 28 last night. It was delayed only about 11 hours by being addressed Bar Harbor, <u>Pennsylvania</u>. I am very glad to hear you think Louise looking a little better. This morning, I have heard from her and as her last two letters seem to have been written in better spirits, I think she must be feeling a little better. I feel very anxious @ [about] her and am awfully glad she is going out to you in good time. She writes much of how good and kind you have been to her – not startling news….[20]

Though Louise was vivacious, talented and industrious, she seemed in frail health even before their marriage, and therefore Ronald was glad that she had been invited to "go out" to stay with the MacDonald's at Casa Coraggio for the winter. He knew that Louise would not only benefit from Bordighera's healthy climate, but also from the loving care that his mother and sisters would give her, especially considering that Louise's own mother had passed away just five years earlier. Ronald further writes in his letter from Bar Harbor:

> I leave here next Saturday Sept. 17. I shall stay a few days at Hartford, Connecticut with Mr. & Mrs. Keller (Miss Mary Monteith Smith @ whom you and I used to disagree) as they have invited me, then a few days in N.Y. I think, and reach Pottstown (address to Hill School, Pottstown, Pa.) on Sept. 26, school beginning on 28th. It was to have opened on 21st but Meigs[21] has had to add a week to the holidays. Mrs. Scott[22] has been most generous to me and insists on paying my passage from England. I thus shall be able to pay Uncle George and Uncle William at once, with a slight margin left. Also very

---

20 Letter from Ronald MacDonald to Louisa MacDonald dated Sept. 13, 1887 – George MacDonald Collection. General Collection, Beinecke Rare Book and Manuscript Library, Yale University.

21 John Meigs – Headmaster of Hill School, Pottstown, Pa.

22 Probably Mrs. A. J. Scott, widow of family friend Mr. Alexander John Scott, former principal Owens College, Manchester, England.

soon after I hope to be able to work off my few outstanding Oxford debts.[23]

Ronald was looking forward to his new position at Hill School, but he was especially anxious to be rid of his tutoring position. He writes in the same letter:

> I have little to tell you of myself. I have been on very fair terms with the boy, who likes me personally, I think, but not my office. I have let him alone until he come to me, and in this way have been more successful than I hoped when I last wrote. It has been, however, on the whole a disappointing business. The girl is a little horror and tho' I can manage her rather better than anyone else-that is not saying much. [...] I often feel, after teaching her after an hour or two, as if life were a bad, not a good thing. I shall soon, I hope, from Pottstown be able to write more interesting letters.[24]

Ronald arrived at Pottstown in the fall of 1887 to begin his teaching position. Hill School was founded in 1851 by Rev. Matthew Meigs as a "family boarding school" where students lived together with faculty, the first of its kind in the country. By Ronald's time, the headmastership had been turned over to the founder's son, John Meigs, who had rescued the fledgling school from ruin. When John Meigs first became headmaster in 1876, the school had but a dozen students and only one or two masters. By 1887, when Ronald arrived the school had a faculty of nine or ten with a student body of seventy-five boys. The school campus had also been improved. "Professor" Meigs (so-called to distinguish him from his father, Dr. Meigs) and his dear wife "Mrs. John," were not only dearly loved by the staff and boys, but in their 35 year career in the headmastership of the school, put the school on a firm foundation for future growth.

It seems to be a mystery as to how Ronald heard about the Hill School, as there is no record in the family correspondence of his contact with the school prior to his leaving for America in September 1887. However, Meigs' biographer tells us that "In the summer of 1887, he [John Meigs] took three Hill boys with him to England, for four weeks'

23 Letter from Ronald MacDonald to Louisa MacDonald dated Sept. 13, 1887 – George MacDonald Collection. General Collection, Beinecke Rare Book and Manuscript Library, Yale University.

24 Ibid.

vacation…."[25] The fact that he took three boys with him, and that the biographer records that they visited such places as Thomas Arnold's famous school at Rugby and Eton College, makes us surmise that one of the purposes of the "vacation" was to promote The Hill School. It's certainly plausible to think that Meigs, who was always on the lookout for quality university-trained Christian teachers to maintain the high ideals of his school, may have met up with Ronald that summer, as it was that September that Ronald first sailed for America.

HILL SCHOOL FACULTY 1888-89. RONALD MACDONALD TOP ROW, FAR RIGHT
COURTESY, HILL SCHOOL, POTTSTOWN, PA.

At first Ronald enjoyed his new position, though he keenly felt the loneliness of being far from his family. In a letter dated October 25, 1887 to his sister Winifred, after wishing her a happy birthday and "many happy returns" he laments: "The only happy returns here are Sundays and holidays." He resumes a more positive outlook later in the letter when he writes:

---

25   Walter Russell Bowie, *The Master of the Hill: A Biography of John Meigs.* (New York: Dodd, Mead and Company, 1917), p.121.

> As you may have heard, I like the boss here very much. But I see little of him now, as we are both very busy. For a fortnight I sat next him at table and we had good fun together. But now I dispense to a rather stupid lot of big boys. I play football hard every afternoon, with no glory, but many bruises. [...] Tell Louise to give you a kiss for me, and give her one from me.[26]

Ronald remained at Hill School for the scholastic year 1887-88, and returned to England after the Spring term to marry his beloved Louise. They wed on July 7, 1888 in Hendon, London. Shortly thereafter they spent their newlywed days in Littlehampton, a seaside town on the southern coast of England (a short distance from Arundel, the city where George MacDonald had his first and only pastorate.) During their stay, Ronald's sister Lilia, who was born in Arundel, went down from London for a visit and wrote back to her mother Louisa:

> I got down here alright, & was met by Ronald & Louise – they have got very nice rooms, & seem extremely happy. She is looking well for her. – It is very nice down here and the country round is charming – We went for a lovely drive this morning- we talked of Arundel, but the weather was too unsettled so they mean to do that on their way back on Tuesday – They came here because they thought Broadstairs wd. be too cold this weather[?] – & Ronald remembered it as a quiet place when he was a child – I can not fit any of the place with what I remember.[27]

The young couple's honeymoon days only lasted for the summer as Ronald was due back to Hill School to teach in the Fall term of 1888.

---

26 Letter from Ronald MacDonald to Winifred MacDonald dated October 25, 1887 – George MacDonald Collection. General Collection, Beinecke Rare Book and Manuscript Library, Yale University.

27 Letter from Lilia MacDonald to Louisa MacDonald 1888 – George MacDonald Collection. General Collection, Beinecke Rare Book and Manuscript Library, Yale University.

> Potts Corner.
>
> Nov. 1888   Penn.
>
>   U.S.A.

My Dearest Winnie,

        Though we were bad enough not to write to you for the sixth, still we did think lovingly of you on that day – + had many loving wishes in our hearts for you – + it is better to tell you so late than not at all – isn't it? I thought much of you too, when I unpacked all the things you had packed with me – at St. John Lee, + longed to be able to see you sometimes. It is so dreadful to be quite cut off from you all, + I miss you very very much. I wonder if you will flourish +thrive on Bordighera air as you did last.

FRONT PAGE OF LETTER FROM LOUISE VIRENDA MACDONALD
TO WINIFRED MACDONALD, NOVEMBER 1888.
COURTESY BEINECKE LIBRARY, YALE UNIVERSITY

❖ Chapter 3 ❖

NEWLYWEDS IN AMERICA

Not only did Ronald come to America before 1889, but the family letters reveal that he also took his bride with him when he returned to America that Fall of 1888. Louise reveals this herself in the only extant letter we have from her. In the letter, dated November 1888 to her sister-in-law Winifred, with "Pottstown, Penn. U.S.A." written at the top, Louise writes:

> Though we were bad enough not to write to you for the sixth [Winifred's birthday], still we did think lovingly of you on that day – & had many loving wishes in our hearts for you – & it is better to tell you so late than not at all-isn't it? I thought much of you too, when I unpacked all the things you had packed with me at St. John Lee, & longed to be able to see you sometimes. This is so dreadful to be cut off from you all, & miss you very much. I wonder if you will flourish and strive on Bordighera air as you did last winter. I have great longing for Bordighera often, & think much of you there – & can smell the pines, and fancy I am drinking in the lovely air. I often wonder whether Ronald & I will ever see the place again! When we are old and grey perhaps.[28]

Although Louise was an American citizen, having been born in Baltimore to an American mother and having lived in America as a young child, she considered England her home. In fact to her, America was a foreign country. Her letter from Pottstown shows this, as she continues to Winifred:

---

28 Letter from Louise Virenda Blandy MacDonald to Winifred MacDonald dated November 1888 – George MacDonald Collection. General Collection, Beinecke Rare Book and Manuscript Library, Yale University.

Ronald & I bear our exile but ill & we both feel that any hole or corner in England, even in the black country, would be preferable to the loveliest place to be found in all America. We live in hopes of coming back to England to live, somehow and somewhen – I do not think we shall ever be reconciled to this banishment, it is utterly hateful to us both. I can't describe the feeling I have here towards everything English – even to a scrap of paper or bit of string, & I am consumed by envy of all those happy people who can live at home. This is indeed a fine sort of birthday letter to write you! But Ronald's is nice to make up for it, & you must fancy that all he has said is half from me, & that this is meant as an echo to it. […] Forgive my grumbling & do not think me thankless of the blessing of being able to be with Ronald, that is of course, the only thing that makes life here bearable.[29]

Louise was not only suffering from homesickness, but also was in shock from the change of culture. For most of her childhood, Louise lived with her family in the high society of London. Her father, a well known dentist with an office in prestigious Harley Street, London was quite well-to-do and raised his family in his affluence. In fact, the local 1871 census recorded that Dr. Blandy was not only providing a living for he and his wife and six children, but was also housing his widowed mother-in-law, two unmarried sisters-in-law, and six servants. The demographics of England during the nineteenth-century were similar to that of the United States with the northern sections of the country having mostly industrialized, middle-class cities such as Manchester, Blackburn and Liverpool, and the southern sections represented by the upper-class society with their Country Estates and Townhomes.

Pottstown was a cultural antithesis to the high-society urbanized "southern" cities (Baltimore & London) to which Louise was accustomed. Pottstown, was originally founded around "Pottsgrove Manor," an early iron furnace, and by 1888, the railroad had brought easy access to coal along with ease of shipping finished products which resulted in a "boom" to the town's population and number of iron factories.[30] At the time that the MacDonalds lived there, Pottstown

---

29 Ibid.

30 TriCounty Area Chamber of Commerce – *www.tricountyareachamber.com/pages/areahistory-pottstown.asp.*

was a small sooty, industrialized town. John Meigs' biographer, Walter Russell Bowie, in 1917 in describing the area writes:

> "The valley of the Schuylkill [river] is naturally a pleasant country, of gentle undulations and not infertile lands, green and fair to look upon; but its great iron deposits have called into being along the river huge iron foundries that have given character to the towns. They are industrial communities, with an industrial population, and an industrial aspect. One would never now deliberately pick out Pottstown as the natural site for a great school, for there is little in the town itself which suggests scholastic quiet and mellow atmosphere of meditation."[31]

Edith Darrach, a dear friend whom Ronald & Louise had befriended at Hill School, gives us more insight into their situation. Mrs. Darrach, who had two sons at Hill School, was "matron of the whole school, whose sweet and ardent nature comforted many a lonely boy."[32] This sweet but perceptive woman quickly assessed the situation and just as she comforted "many a lonely boy," she took Ronald & Louise under her matronly wings. In a letter sent long after the MacDonalds had left Pottstown, addressed to Ronald's sister Lilia at Ravenscroft in December of 1890, Mrs. Darrach writes:

> In the first days of your brother's life in Pottstown, so dreary & well nigh intolerable as they were to him, it was my privilege to see a good deal of him[…]. I do not need to tell you what a rare treat it has been to me to be allowed to know and love your brother and his wife. It is one of the greatest blessings of my life. I think often that I could show you Louise in quite a new and different light. Could I tell you of her life in this dreary wretched little town. Her surroundings were most uninteresting-often most trying – but as I look back on the hours I have spent with them in their own tiny quarters – I realize that I owe to her as well as to him what I can never overestimate. The nobility-the transparent purity – the exquisite grace of her character were marvelous – and I love her for what she was, and for what she did for me the more as I continue to realize its withdrawal.[33]

31   Walter Russell Bowie, *The Master of the Hill: A Biography of John Meigs.* (New York: Dodd, Mead and Company, 1917), pp. 22-23.

32   F. M. Huntington Wilson, *The Memoirs of An Ex-Diplomat.* (Boston: Bruce Humphries, Inc., 1945), p.28.

33   Letter from Emily Romeyn Darrach to Lilia MacDonald – December 20, 1890 – George MacDonald Collection. General Collection, Beinecke Rare Book and Manuscript Library, Yale University.

Ronald & Louise did eventually make friends and settle into the life of the school. In fact we know that Louise was able to continue her drawing while at Pottstown. While at Hill School, she executed an almost photographic image of the school's founder, Rev. Matthew Meigs. The drawing now hangs at the University of Delaware where Meigs was president in 1851 prior to founding Hill School.

REV. MATTHEW MEIGS
DRAWING BY LOUISE MACDONALD
COURTESY, HILL SCHOOL, POTTSTOWN, PA.

HILL SCHOOL STUDENTS & FACULTY 1888-89
RONALD — TOP ROW, FIFTH FROM THE RIGHT
COURTESY HILL SCHOOL, POTTSTOWN, PA

"THE COTTAGE" AT HILL SCHOOL — C.1880S. RONALD AND
LOUISE'S "TINY QUARTERS" WERE PROBABLY IN THIS BUILDING.
COURTESY, HILL SCHOOL, POTTSTOWN, PA.

HILL SCHOOL DINING ROOM IN 1914

HILL SCHOOL CLASSROOM

28

RavenScroft 1881 (view from Swannanoa Hotel)
DALE SLUSSER COLLECTION

❖ CHAPTER 4 ❖

GOING SOUTH

It is not surprising that by the spring of 1889 after a term or two at Hill School Ronald was looking for a change of situation. Also by this time Louise was pregnant and about to deliver their first child, which doubtless was taxing to her already frail constitution. So Ronald, in an effort to find a better situation for himself and his wife, considered opening his own school in Alabama. On May 14, 1889, upon hearing of Ronald's idea, George MacDonald writes from Bordighera to his wife:

> A delightful letter from Virenda – Ronald is thinking of starting a school in Alabama-for himself – but doubtless you'll hear about it from Greville – He is to have the telegraph about the baby – and he is to telegraph to us. I'll send her delightful letter tomorrow – she is delighted with the baby clothes…[34]

Ronald's scheme was not very popular with his family, as four days later his father again writes to his mother about the matter:

> I lunched with Greville yesterday. […] He is set against Ronald's going to Alabama. Mr. Binney [George's first cousin's husband] is dead set against it too. Bad climate & bad society. We all think he can do better at home. It is nearly a tropical climate. Greville will raise £500 by insuring his life, & I will raise £500 somehow to start him in a school at home. Greville is going to telegraph as much to him. I think, it would be a far worse separation then where he is now.[35]

---

34 Letter from George MacDonald to Louisa MacDonald – May 14, 1889 – George MacDonald Collection. General Collection, Beinecke Rare Book and Manuscript Library, Yale University.

35 Letter from George MacDonald to Louisa MacDonald- May 18, 1889 – George MacDonald Collection. General Collection, Beinecke Rare Book and Manuscript Library, Yale University.

Although the family was successful in persuading Ronald against moving to Alabama, they were unsuccessful in getting him to move back to England, as he soon accepted a position as the headmaster at the Ravenscroft High School for Boys in Asheville, North Carolina in the summer of 1889. However, Ronald & Louise did return to England for a few months that summer before Ronald began his new position. I believe the young couple went home to show off their new baby girl, Ozella Louise MacDonald (who I surmise was born that spring in Pottstown). Ozella was named after Louise's mother and sister. Interestingly, her sister Ozella Jane Blandy passed away that same year (1889) at the age of 38. We have record of the couple's visit to England in a letter from Ronald's mother to his father. Louisa MacDonald writes to George MacDonald from Richmond, London on August 19, 1889:

> Ronald and Louise seem depressed as the time for parting gets so near. I have sent MacKay [Ronald's brother] up to Hampstead to buy a bottle of Port for Virenda [Louise], the ale has not suited her the last 2 days.[36]

Their brief return to England was also verified by the report of Rev. D. H. Buel, secretary of the Board of Fellows of Ravenscroft, to the 1890 Convention of the Episcopal Diocese of North Carolina. Speaking of possible reasons for the low numbers of boys attending that year, Buel reports: "Mr. McDonald [sic] was obliged to be absent several weeks last summer in England and could not reach Asheville until very near the time of the opening of the school...."[37]

In a small valley plateau of the Blue Ridge Mountains in western North Carolina is the city of Asheville. In its early days, being only accessible from any direction by traversing a mountain, it was nothing more than a way station for "drovers" who would stop there with their herds and flocks of livestock on the their way down the mountain to lowland markets. But all that changed one day in 1880 when the train reached Asheville from the east. Soon railroad lines from all directions were built and Asheville was changed forever. Once virtually unknown, Asheville's scenic beauty, moderate climate and fresh mountain air drew

---

36 Letter from Louisa MacDonald to George MacDonald – August 19, 1889 – George MacDonald Collection. General Collection, Beinecke Rare Book and Manuscript Library, Yale University.

37 Journal of the Seventy-fourth Annual Convention of the Diocese of North Carolina, 1890; p. 69.

both tourists and permanent residents. In fact, the railroad worked along with Asheville's Chamber of Commerce to drum up business; together they began what we would call today an "ad campaign" in the form of numerous booklets and travelogues and magazine advertisements. One such booklet of 1892 reads:

> This "Sky-Land," this city of refuge alike from the blizzards of northern winters , and the sultry southern summer's sun, where her children may hold high carnival, where the winters are softened, and where the summers are fanned by high breezes fresh from the mountains, and where the weary may rest in an all year jubilee.[38]

With advertisements like that, it is not surprising that within a decade of the railroad arriving Asheville's population grew from 2,500 in 1880 to almost 12,000 by 1890.[39] The rapid increase in population combined with 100,000 yearly visitors, caused the city to scrambled to provide for the massive and rapid growth. By 1892 it boasted such amenities as a telephone exchange, a good system of sewage, an efficient fire department, a progressive mayor and city council, five banks, the handsomest opera house in the state, a score of eminent and skillful physicians, excellent schools (both public and private), two large and well equipped tuberculin sanitariums, an electric streetcar railway (the first in the country), two electric light companies, and a well conducted hospital with an efficient medical corps."[40]

Ravenscroft High School, to which Ronald and Louise were bound, had been an established institution in Asheville for many years. Rev. Jarvis Buxton, first rector of Trinity Episcopal Church, Asheville, gives the following account of the school in his *Sketches of Church History*, written in 1892:

> "The Institution at Asheville [...] consisting of two independent departments, provided for in separate buildings, some distance apart, viz: the High School for boys, and the Training School for the ministry. As far back as 1855, the convention [Episcopal Diocese of North Carolina] resolved to establish and locate a High School for boys in Pittsboro'. The Committee in

---

38 Sawyer, Harriet Adams, *Asheville or the Sky-Land*, St. Louis: Nixon-Jones Printing, 1892), p. 10.

39 Ibid, p.17

40 Ibid.

charge afterward changed the location of the school to the town of Asheville. In 1856, it was formally announced by the Headmaster, who was also Rector of the Parish Church at Asheville, that the doors of the Institution were opened for the admission of pupils, and that its aim and purpose was not only to furnish facilities of study to older youth who might have the ministry directly in view, but also to educate the boys of the Church in the method of the Prayer Book and in all Christian culture. At the close of the Civil War, and on the restoration of peace, the Ravenscroft Institute was re-organized by Bishop Atkinson solely into a Theological School, that is, a school where postulants and candidates only for the Holy Ministry, were received and instructed. As a school for boys, in general, it fell in abeyance till of late years. In the year 1886, it was decided by the Convention to revive the plan of a Diocesan School for boys, (the proposed one to be located near Morganton, having miscarried) and to fit up and use for that purpose the Ravenscroft building. The erection of a separate building for the Training School for the Ministry, was postponed to a future day. But a kind Providence came to the rescue, in the generous aid of the late Mr. Schoenberger, a warm personal friend of Bishop Lyman's who, at the cost of $11,000 erected a substantial brick building, known as "Schoenberger Hall," on the grounds of Ravenscroft, for the Training School. The Principals of Ravenscroft have been, Rev. J. Buxton, Rev. Lucian Holmes, Rev. George Wilmer, Rev. F. J. Murdock, Rev. D. H. Buel, now at the head of the Training School for the Ministry. Within the last year [1889] the original Ravenscroft building, used for the High School for boys, has been leased to Mr. McDonald [sic] Headmaster, for a term of five years, free of rent. All that it needs for success under such a Master, is the sympathy and support of the Diocese."[41]

What Rev. Jarvis does not mention in his account is that the re-organized "Ravenscroft High School for Boys" first opened in the Fall of 1887 with Henry A. Prince as headmaster. Prince was replaced within the year by his assistant, Haywood Parker, who carried the headmastership for the next year and a half until Ronald came in the

---

41   Joint Centennial Convention. *Sketches of Church History in North Carolina*, Wilmington, NC: Wm. L. De Rosset, Jr., Publisher, 1892), p. 308-312.

Fall of 1889.

Though no family correspondence reveals how Ronald heard about the Ravenscroft position, the following account from a report to the North Carolina Episcopal Convention of 1890 gives the sequence of events:

> The Board of Fellows of Ravenscroft respectfully report to the Convention, that at a special meeting held during the session of the last Diocesan Convention [mid-May 1889], the Secretary of the Board was instructed to correspond with Mr. Ronald MacDonald, who had been highly recommended to the Board as a very suitable person for the vacant Headmastership of the High School for boys, with the view to obtaining him for that position. This was immediately done, and Mr. MacDonald expressed his willingness to come on, as we wished him to do, to see the place and confer with the committee. This he did at his earliest convenience – and not long after his return home he sent his acceptance of the position on the same terms as Mr. Prince [former Headmaster].[42]

---

42 Journal of the Seventy-fourth Annual Convention of the Diocese of North Carolina, 1890; p. 68.

RAVENSCROFT CAMPUS 1891 - Birdseye View

CHAPTER 5

GOOD NEWS – BAD NEWS

How fortunate Ronald must have felt in the early summer of 1889, for he not only recently became a new father, but he had just obtained a headmastership in a place noted for its fresh air and restorative powers with a healthier climate for his frail wife.

The July 30, 1889 edition of Asheville's newspaper, *The Daily Citizen*, carried a small article on its front page announcing Ronald's appointment:

> We learn with pleasure that the Board of Fellows of Ravenscroft have secured as headmaster of that institution Ronald MacDonald, B.A. He is the son [of] the distinguished writer George MacDonald; is a graduate of Oxford University; has taught most acceptably in some of the public schools of England, and subsequently has for several years taught with equal credit in one of the leading schools of this country. He comes with the best recommendations from the foremost educators in England, and with very strong recommendation from that most eminent educator of youth, Rev. Dr. Henry A. Colt, of St. Paul's Concord, New Hampshire. Those who have long known him speak emphatically of his genial intercourse with boys joined with firmness in maintaining proper discipline. We believe that the school under the headship of Mr. MacDonald, aided as he will be, by competent assistants, will afford the very highest educational advantages and must prove an assured success.[43]

---

43 *The Daily Citizen*. – Tuesday, July 30,1889-front page. – Microfilm: Pack Library, Asheville, NC.

Little correspondence survives from that first year at Ravenscroft, but from the previously mentioned convention report, we learn that he had sixteen boys, with three of them being boarding students. He also is reported to have taken on some improvements to the building and grounds. The Bishop was so encouraged that in January 1890, after only one term, he offered to Ronald to take on a five year lease of the school, with Ronald paying all expenses and receiving all the income. Ronald accepted the offer. So though still under the diocese's oversight, Ronald now had "his own school."

However, all was not as rosy as indicated from the published reports. In a letter of October 18, 1889, Ronald's mother Louisa writes to his father:

> Thank you for yours [letter] with Virenda's. Oh! Don't we know what she went thro' with anxiety about that darling[…]. How brave and sweet she is – isn't she? She's a real mother I'm sure. – Poor little pet. What slow work it will be for them won't it. But it seems as if the pupils are sure to come only they'll want Louise."[44]

By the next summer, after only one year at Ravenscroft, it was apparent that Louise's health was failing and that the young couple needed help. Ronald was now having to run a school, provide for the boarding students, care for his infant daughter, and nurse his very ill wife. The MacDonalds supplied the funds[45] to send Louise's younger sister, Winnie,[46] to be with Louise and help with the housekeeping. Winnie, who was barely 21, set out for America at the end of June, and arrived in Asheville about a week later, laden with gifts, including a "tea gown," which Ronald's mother had had made for Louise. Ronald writes home to his mother on July 9, 1890, of Winnie's arrival. Although he writes of how happy he is, he reveals alarming news of

---

44   Letter from Louisa MacDonald to George MacDonald – October 18, 1889 – George MacDonald Collection. General Collection, Beinecke Rare Book and Manuscript Library, Yale University

45   Although the Blandy family had been affluent, by this time (1890) they had suffered a number of losses. In 1881 Dr. Blandy went bankrupt and soon thereafter in 1882, his wife died. The MacDonalds, always mindful of the needs of others, knew that Winnie would be a comfort to her sister Louise, as well as Ronald.

46   Winnie was her nickname. Her full name was "Varina Anne Jefferson Davis Blandy"– being named after Jefferson & Varina Davis, who lived with the Blandys in 1869, the year of Winnie's birth. See Appendix A.

Louise's condition:

> Dearest Mammy,
>
> It was lovely and therefore like you to send Winnie to us. She came to us beaming like a dear sunbeam this afternoon. How glad Louise is you can only imagine. I feel happier than I have felt for months. I am awfully fond of her to begin with, & then she is just exactly what we need – always plucky happy & opinioned & enthusiastic.
>
> The last three days Louise has seemed less well-has been downright hysterical over her meals, crying over every mouthful, & begging always off, & generally carrying on. This is partly from anxiety about Winnie & the intense excitement her coming has caused her. Now she is here I hope it will be better. I have had an awful time, for she can hardly bear me out of her sight & I have heaps of things to attend to.
>
> It is remarkable how her digestion has improved of late. She has taken her milk pure, & raw eggs without consequent nausea & her dinner even without bad effects. But her nervousness & readiness to cry have been fearfully distressing. She has slept very badly, but better last night. The day before yesterday & today she had long drives, & I have hired a carriage & pair for a week to drive her myself every day. The air, the weather, the scenery, and the smell of the pines here are all glorious....[47]

The middle of the letter contains a long description of some of the servants, he had hired to help with the manual duties around the house and school. After that he again thanks his mother for sending Winnie, and then he opens up, revealing his inner struggles with his situation:

> Dearest Mother,
>
> How shall we thank you for your great & untiring goodness to us. It was so good of you to send our dear sister, & money (which I must keep, for dear wife's sake) & heaps of nice things. When I think-you have been thro' all this, & God knows more, with father, I know how you must feel with me, & indeed fancy that from it I can gather better knowledge of my mother & father that I so love & worship. Mammy dear, I am so often

---

47 Letter from Ronald MacDonald to Louisa MacDonald – July 9, 1890 – George MacDonald Collection. General Collection, Beinecke Rare Book and Manuscript Library, Yale University

little credit to you, & my temper is sometimes abominable. I never openly lose it in official relations – with boys, master, or servants, but they have all tried me, & housekeeper & parents have nearly driven me wild & constant attendance on Louise & keeping indoors has driven me sometimes to my wits end. God helps me through all these troubles wonderfully, but I sometimes think that if I should lose Louise, I should never do any more good work....[48]

Upon receiving the letter and after waiting to see if there is any more news, Louisa, who is in Wainsford, England while her husband is there on a lecture tour, forwards Ronald's letter to her daughter Lily, with an accompanying letter:

My Dearest Lilia,

I could not bear to part with this letter directly it came, it seemed too sad and I could not bear either sending such a sad news to you sooner than perhaps there was any occasion for, but nothing else seems to come, at present, to bring more hope and you ought to know, but please dear send me the letter back again when you have read it.

Is it not terribly sad for our dear Ronald, so alone, so dreary for him! And it does seem to me that the end must be very near, from this letter. And another bad sign is, that I have not had a word from Winnie Blandy, who promised to write her true opinion, though she said, "if I think badly of her, am I to say exactly what I think? Well! I will remember what you say, but I don't believe I should be able to send you a bad account – I know I could not write it." – And not having had one word from her, I fear she has not really the heart to write to me.

[…] Father says that if he [Ronald] is left and the worst should happen before he goes out to Bordighera he will go to Asheville to him, and I should like him to do that very much."[49]

As alarming as Ronald's first letter seemed, the next letter that he wrote, less than a week later, sounded the final alarm. Even the change in his handwriting in this letter, reflected Ronald's overwhelming

---

48 Ibid.

49 Letter from Louisa MacDonald to Lilia MacDonald – July 31, 1890 – George MacDonald Collection. General Collection, Beinecke Rare Book and Manuscript Library, Yale University

melancholy. I quote this revealing letter in its entirety:

My darling Mother,

I am going away tomorrow with Louise for a change to a nice farm boarding-house with Louise. Her doctor wants her to go, & have been to see the place & like [it]. But I fear it will do her no good. I wish I were not bound in honor to stay here, & I would bring [her] to Bordighera for the winter, though I fear she is already too weak for the journey. I am nearly heart-broken but God is very good to me. All your unspeakable kindness & father's beautiful letter have given me much comfort. But it is so hard to see her suffer. If I lost her I should have to suffer, but I am not allowed to bear her weakness and pain. Winnie is very good, but sweetly comforting & helpful as she is to us both, I fear she has only come to a very sad house. We keep very happy with Louise, but I feel awfully tired, & break down horribly when I am away from my darling. In spite of her thinness, she looks most exquisitely lovely in her tea gown, you sent her. Dear Mammy, pray for me. It is curious that in this my greatest trouble I feel God's goodness & presence more sweetly & closely than ever before – thanks be to him. And yet I suffer awfully. Your loving son, Ronald

– I will write to father in a day or two. I would I had Greville to doctor & Lily to nurse."[50]

Now it was evident that Ronald needed more help, so his mother and father decide that his sister Lily should be the one to go America to help Ronald. Louisa writes to Lily:

Dearest Lilia,

We have had the most distressing letter from Ronald, and it has come very strongly into father's and my minds that you are dear, the only one of us that can give the consolation – the only consolation there is to be given, of your personal sympathy and presence, should you mind going dearest one, to him when MacKay and Irene come over here? Could you not go to him, his school will be opening about then and if she is getting worse, it will be so sad for him to have to leave her so much. If he knew you were there that would make it a little easier. You

---

50 Letter from Ronald MacDonald to Louisa MacDonald – July 15, 1890 – George MacDonald Collection. General Collection, Beinecke Rare Book and Manuscript Library, Yale University

see he said once, and that was after W. B. [Winnie Blandy] had gone there, "If only you or Lily could be here to help nurse her, and to speak to Me!"!! And then if after all there were some hope that Bordighera would or might do her some good, and if she would go without him, I know you would not mind going with her, would you dear? By the Florio line, which we hear is a very good line from New York to Genoa[…] And then 'dear which I think is much the most likely, that she will be too ill to be moved and if she is going to leave him quickly, if you were there, you see from this lovely, touching letter, that that would be a comfort to him, poor boy, for indeed he is still one for all his manly goodness and tender care of her. How terribly hard it is for him and will be worse. – But if we could spare you for a month or two dear, well we are making the only sacrifice we could and I know you're willing because you said once you would like to go to him…[51]

Louisa's persistent and persuasive letter convinced Lilia to go. Lilia replies on August, from Italy, with enthusiasm:

[…] I can't say how grateful I shall be to go to them – I quite <u>longed</u> to be with them both, only I thought it wd. be such an expense for you- I think the dear boy wd. sooner have me than any one after you & Father. […]Then I feel that it wd. be much to us all to feel that one of his own was with dear Ronald…[52]

Lilia wants to go right away instead of waiting until MacKay & Irene (her brother and sister) go back to England in September, as her mother suggests. Lilia writes back in the same letter that Irene is much better. Lilia feels so strongly about this that she writes a second note, dated the same day, imploring her mother:

[…] I feel so sorry that I am not to go at once, that, at the risk of being tiresome, I do beg you dear darling Mammy to reconsider your decision – I feel so strongly that <u>now</u> is the time I shd. be of use to him just as his school-term is commencing & he, <u>must</u> be more away from dear Virenda, it would be a comfort (for the hour) to him to know I was with her..[53]

51 Letter from Louisa MacDonald to Lilia MacDonald – August 9, 1890 – George MacDonald Collection. General Collection, Beinecke Rare Book and Manuscript Library, Yale University

52 Letter from Lilia MacDonald to Louisa MacDonald – August 13, 1890 – George MacDonald Collection. General Collection, Beinecke Rare Book and Manuscript Library, Yale University

53 Letter from Lilia MacDonald to Louisa MacDonald – August 13, 1890 – George MacDonald

Apparently Louisa's persistence won out, as Lilia did not leave England until early September. On September 2, while staying with a family friend, James Sing, in Liverpool, where I believe she was to board the ship to America, she received a short note from her Father:

> I have thought of something to send you out of my waist-coat pocket – a valuable coin of the year you were born. I hope the post office will let it pass. My love to you all the voyage and to all eternity, forever and always. When you feel ill think how happy Ronald will be to see you. One of the handkerchiefs in the box your mother sends him is one of those Mr. Wylde gave me with my initials. Give my dear love. Nothing else is any good. Your loving father.

The next day Lilia boards the "S. S. City of New York"[54] ocean liner bound for New York City with an intermediate stop in Queenstown,

S. S. City of New York

Ireland. James Sing has not only given her a lot of advice about traveling, such as currency exchange and recommending a sleeping cabin, but also he had arranged for her to dine at the captain's table where she met some interesting people. Lilia uses the solitude on the ship to write a long letter which she posts from Queenstown. She writes of

Collection. General Collection, Beinecke Rare Book and Manuscript Library, Yale University
54 This is conjecture on my part-but it matches her letter dates. The S. S. City of New York left Liverpool and sailed to Queenstown where it stopped on September 4, 1890 arriving in New York on September 10. – see www.norwayheritage.com/p_ship.asp?sh=ciny3.

the trivialities of ship life, like how grand the ship is with its beautiful electric lights and she describes the people on board and their various idiosyncrasies. But for Lilia, the ever-giving servant, ship life is a time of welcome respite:

> Dear dear love to all & everyone – you know how much I shall be thinking of you all, & wishing you had some of my enforced leisure – It is such a curious sensation that no one wants me or cares a rap what I do.[55]

LILIA SCOTT MACDONALD
COURTESY BEINECKE LIBRARY, YALE UNIVERSITY

---

55   Letter from Lilia MacDonald to Louisa MacDonald – September 3, 1890 – George MacDonald Collection. General Collection, Beinecke Rare Book and Manuscript Library, Yale University

CHAPTER 6

A LATE COMFORT

Lilia did not know before boarding the ship that it was already too late for her to provide any comfort, for Louise had died on Wednesday, August 27, 1890. The evening edition of *The Daily Citizen* carried the following notice on its front page:

> Louise Virenda, wife of Ronald McDonald, of Ravenscroft school, died suddenly this morning. Mrs. MacDonald had been in poor health for sometime, but her death will be a sad surprise to her many friends. She was a member of the Episcopal church, an earnest and faithful worker, and beloved by all who knew her. Notice of the funeral will be given later."[56]

The next evening, in its "Around Town" column, the newspaper printed this short notice: "The funeral services of the late Mrs. Louise V. MacDonald were held this afternoon at Trinity Church by the Rev. Jarvis Buxton,"[57] Her body was laid to rest at Riverside Cemetery, northwest of Asheville.[58]

Though we have no letter from Ronald himself describing the scene of those last days of his beloved, we get a glimpse into his heart through one of his novels, written almost twenty years later. Describing the deathbed scene, where the main character of the story is dying and leaving behind a beloved wife and infant boy, Ronald writes:

---

56   *The Daily Citizen.* – Wednesday, August 27,1890 – front page. – Microfilm: Pack Library, Asheville, NC.

57   *The Daily Citizen.* – Thursday, August 28, 1890 – front page. – Microfilm: Pack Library, Asheville, NC.

58   I discovered her grave through cemetery records – Section F Lot 19. – All that remains (or all that was ever erected) are two granite bases marking the gravesite.

In such an hour, a man's heart, be he the sick or the whole, will tell him: "This is the time for saying and hearing all that has never yet been heard nor said between us. This is the moment when passion may distil its finest essence. In the near loss of everything but our spiritual relation we may know, perhaps, and touch each other with an intimacy never yet attained— reaching, for a moment before the last curtain falls between, almost to the secret of that eternal relation which underlies the mystery of man and woman."[59]

A few days after the funeral, a small notice appeared in the town newspaper, under the heading "Ravenscroft School," which read:

> An impression prevails to some extent that the recent death of Mrs. MacDonald, wife of the principal of the above institution, will influence the movement of Mr. MacDonald in connection with it. We are authorized to say that there will be no change in its management, and it will be continued as heretofore under present conditions. The loss of matronly supervision of Mrs. MacDonald will be appropriately supplied.[60]

What a welcome sight it must have been for Ronald to greet his sister Lilia when she stepped off the train in Asheville a few weeks later. After resting a few days, Lilia writes a lengthy letter home to her mother describing her travels including a grueling ride on an overdue (10 hrs.) train, and other general news. But most importantly, she reports of Ronald's state of mind and physical condition:

> But I can tell you about Ronald – he came to meet me at 2:30 a.m. on Friday morning. I ought to have arrived Thursday afternoon, & we have been almost incessantly together. He is looking very thin & worn but not ill – His body looks small & shrunk & his head big, his hair so thin & eyes so big and blue – & he does everything, sees to everything, laughs, smokes, & talks, talks, talks, incessantly. I feel in just sitting there & receiving it, I am doing what is very necessary for him – He is absolutely unselfish to everyone & is able to speak of Louise as if she were just away for a time – I mean in connection with all the daily duties & accidents of life in a way that is most nobly

59 Ronald MacDonald, *The Carcase*. (London: Everett & Co., 1909), p.323.

60 *The Daily Citizen*. – September 2, 1890. – Microfilm: NC Collection – Pack Library, Asheville, NC

heroic. – I daresay that will not come so easily to him after the first his school begins on the 15th, & will be so full that he is rather put to it to arrange everything with his small staff. – One of the few times I have seen him breakdown was when I gave him the money from B. & Mrs. F. The great kindness of everyone, wd. if it were possible to over value, he wd., & the success of the school & himself with the tiresome people he has had to manage, are almost more than he can bear when he thinks she shared only his struggles – I don't mean that they did not share the kindnesses – It is most beautiful to hear him talk of her & you can imagine how all the subjects he begins on lead to the <u>one</u> incessantly.[61]

Later on in the same letter, Lilia recounts what she had heard of Louise's last days:

He [Ronald] says no one can tell how he longed for a letter from you the first few days of his loneliness. He has of course told you that they had a very delightful nurse the last week, & the doctor has told him since that he was afraid R[onald] wd. breakdown & that it was partly on his account that he sent for her [the nurse]. He will also have told you of the burial being the next day, & many other things that I may say again in the fear he may not have told you. Her perfect content to go is a great comfort to him – He says that before that, her resignation was so sweet that to & in most people it would have seemed everything, but that it was quite a different thing from what she felt afterward- he says that to have seen the peace and readiness come, was so beautiful to him. Wynnie [Winnie] says Virenda's sorrow was much more for him than for the baby because she was so safe in the knowledge that with you & us & them love would always surround her. [...]So far I have not approached the subject of what R. will do in the future. – He is so worn & so apprehensive about the immediate next few weeks[...]

He sleeps so very badly poor fellow – He went back to her room almost directly – Wynnie encouraging him to do so, as she saw it wd. get almost impossible for him if he left it.[62]

---

61   Letter from Lilia MacDonald to Louisa MacDonald – September 14, 1890 – George MacDonald Collection. General Collection, Beinecke Rare Book and Manuscript Library, Yale University

62   Ibid.

Lilia also sends her mother what every loving grandmother wants to hear: news of her darling granddaughter. The family had not seen Ozella since her birth over a year ago. Lilia gives a lengthy and very elaborate description:

> The baby is indeed a little gem. The gentlest & most gracious little child I ever saw – every movement is full of sedate simplicity & she can hardly move her hands & arms without giving one a sense of benediction. She is small & has the same quaint individual face that she had-very little colour but her complexion a healthy cream just tinged with brown – She is out so much- in the mornings, in the garden. She wears the sweetest little white caps – like a little peasant cap – or a darling night cap – sweet little white frocks & no shoes or socks – I think her brow & eyes very like Louise, & also her serenity. She looks in perfect satisfaction when she is on her father's knee, wh. is by the hour together, & his slightest word checks her, without any hidden expression. She loves gentle little larks with him & is so loving with him. The last few days [of Virenda's life] she clung to her mother in the strangest way, they say. She is cutting a tooth of course – & is very free with her coral & bells[63], giving her father & me long pulls at the coral in turns – She is very pleased with the woolen ball you sent her – I have not heard her fret once for a moment since I came, & only very rarely short & vigorous howling in the distance.[64]

Louisa had written a letter the same day Lilia wrote hers, to tell her husband that she was worried as she had not received a letter from Ronald since Lilia had left to go be with him. So Lilia's long letter home was a welcome relief to her mother. Louisa's next letter to her husband is noteworthy for her motherly reactions:

---

63 A Victorian baby rattle used for teething – the baby would suck on the coral, which was soothing to the gums.

64 Letter from Lilia MacDonald to Louisa MacDonald – September 14, 1890 – George MacDonald Collection. General Collection, Beinecke Rare Book and Manuscript Library, Yale University

Since I wrote last I have had a most charming letter from Lilia. What lovely children we have dearest. Is not Ronald a gem? Surely something grand must come out of him and it seems as if he ought to be in a wider sphere. Some day(s) it does look like waste to my circumscribed vision, to have him long at Asheville with those unmanerly [sic] cubs.[65]

AUTHOR, NEXT TO LOUISE'S GRAVESITE
AT RIVERSIDE CEMETERY, ASHEVILLE, NC.
PHOTO BY JOE FRANKLIN

---

65 Letter from Louisa MacDonald to George MacDonald – Thursday, October 2 (?), 1890- George MacDonald Collection. General Collection, Beinecke Rare Book and Manuscript Library, Yale University

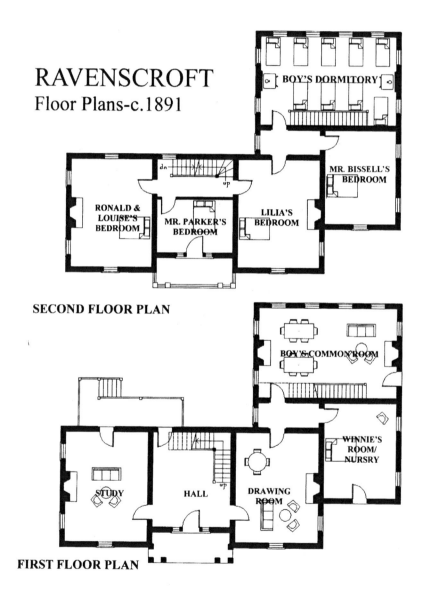

RAVENSCROFT
Floor Plans-c.1891

BOY'S DORMITORY

MR. BISSELL'S
BEDROOM

RONALD &
LOUISE'S
BEDROOM

MR. PARKER'S
BEDROOM

LILIA'S
BEDROOM

SECOND FLOOR PLAN

BOY'S COMMON ROOM

WINNIE'S
ROOM/
NURSRY

STUDY

HALL

DRAWING
ROOM

FIRST FLOOR PLAN

❖ CHAPTER 7 ❖

LIFE AT RAVENSCROFT

We get a good glimpse into life at "Ravenscroft" after Louise's death from letters written home from Lilia, Ronald, and later, Jessie Sharman, Louisa MacDonald's cousin who comes to replace Winnie and Lilia as matron and housekeeper. Lilia gives us a wonderful description of the house and grounds in many of her letters. In one such letter she describes to her Mother:

> The house is so nice & old & queer – a mixture of an old English and Italian house – The big bare bedrooms, the jalousies, the warm air, big open grates & countless doors & noisy stairs are like Italy, & the beautiful old doors and jambs & wooden railings are like a better sort of old farmhouse at home. They have made it so pretty- just in the way your father wd. have done – so simple & dainty & comfortable. – I don't know any outside thing made me feel the sadness [of Virenda's passing] more than all the pretty things so daintily arranged that I knew so well as their wedding presents. – The drawing room is on the right, & Ronald's study on the left of the pretty hall. Both sunny cheerful rooms. The school house is at the foot of the garden [yard] in front – some distance off down a pretty path- that is only for the teaching. The dormitory and common room are in the house.[66]

In a later letter to her brother MacKay she even tells of the furnishings:

> Ronald & Mr. Bissell are making out examination papers at the middle table – one R. made himself with a lower shelf to it – charming! We do everything at it – take tea, feed the baby,

66   Ibid.

play cards, drink beer & hot lemonade, read, write, etc. My own corner as a rule is where I am now, at a round table on a divan to the right of the nice old-fashioned fireplace.[67]

The Ravenscroft building was not just a school, it was also a place where the housekeeping staff, students, masters, headmaster and guests lived, dined, worked and played. These letters reveal that because they all lived and worked together, there was a family-like atmosphere with Ronald at the head. Lilia writes: "– Meals & prayers & school-rooms are all very punctual and no fuss. R[onald] is quite master in his own house & always will be – Noise in the kitchen last night – down he goes – dead silence in half a wink."[68] In another letter, speaking of Ronald being master of the house, Lilia comments: "– Most decided – the servants all like & fear him."[69] Ronald himself, in a letter home to his father, reveals one of the less desirable duties of his headmastership. After telling his father that he had been out sick for ten days, and that things have gotten in arrears, he relates:

> I am not quite strong again yet & quite put out by having a bad boy brought to me. I was keeping him in the study in disgrace, while I sent a note to his father that I must flog or expel him. Father came down to pow-wow, but behaved all right. Execution postponed till tomorrow, when I shall be more up to the job.[70]

Dealing with the housekeeping staff[71] was a daunting task, as unlike in England where servants were highly trained, the servants at Ravenscroft were unreliable and often troublesome. Lilia, accustomed to the proper protocol for British servants, was intrigued and often shocked with her house servants. In a letter Lilia writes about a month

67   Letter from Lilia MacDonald to MacKay MacDonald – December 14, 1890 – George MacDonald Collection. General Collection, Beinecke Rare Book and Manuscript Library, Yale University

68   Letter from Lilia MacDonald to Louisa MacDonald – Wednesday, September 24, 1890 – George MacDonald Collection. General Collection, Beinecke Rare Book and Manuscript Library, Yale University

69   Letter from Lilia MacDonald to Louisa MacDonald – October 15, 1890 – George MacDonald Collection. General Collection, Beinecke Rare Book and Manuscript Library, Yale University

70   Letter from Ronald MacDonald to George MacDonald – October 9 & 18 & 19, 1890 – George MacDonald Collection. General Collection, Beinecke Rare Book and Manuscript Library, Yale University

71   A search of the 1890 Asheville City Directory shows the following staff: Jeff Blair, porter; Lizzie Moorhead, housemaid; Benjamin Lee, coachman; Emma Lee, cook and Annie Bangle, nurse.

after arriving, she gives an account of the state of affairs:

> W.B. [Winnie Blandy] is much distracting me with a voluble
> description of how the nurse dismissed this morning <u>must</u> have
> taken 50 cents out of her drawer.[…] There has been a regular
> clearance today, as she (the nurse) and the man had both to
> be turned away before church time, as they were discovered
> drinking together at 9:00 a.m. by Emma, the cook, […] to the
> several neglect of the horse, the cow & the baby- Jeff was quite
> drunk – such a huge strong man! But another is already engaged
> – When Ronald came in from a ride this afternoon there were
> already other men waiting to be engaged. Ronald says there is
> a sort of freemasonry among them. […] Much modesty and
> patience is required by those who "keep house" you perceive.
> When your housemaid says for you, "Miss Blandy, if you're
> going downstairs, you can take this cup down for me." you feel
> so taken aback that you meekly do as you are told, as Miss B.
> did on that occasion – for which Ronald scolded her well.[72]

Along with the staff, there were boys also living in the dormitory
section of Ravenscroft. Ronald was responsible for their care as well.
Lilia writes of the boys who were boarding at the school that year
(1890): "Of the eight boarders, two are gentleman & have the best
heads – two are tiny boys (one of them always in angry tears) – two
are brothers from a very proper & Y.M.C.A. family whose Mom-ma
w[ouldn't] like them to play cards & who have brought bicycles."[73]

Although most of the descriptions we have of life at Ravenscroft
are from the perspective of the staff, we have one excellent description
from one of the boys, F. M. Huntington Wilson, who was a student
during that time. He tells us:

> "I was sent as a boarder to the Ravenscroft School. There were
> about fourteen boarding pupils in a dormitory with cubicles
> curtained off. All were Southerners but me and the first night,
> after the lights were out, there began a low menacing chorus of
> "Hard times for the Yankees." I got all my shoes up on the bed
> and awaited the attack, but nothing really happened.

---

72 Letter from Lilia MacDonald to MacKay MacDonald- October 5, 1890 – George MacDonald
Collection. General Collection, Beinecke Rare Book and Manuscript Library, Yale University

73 Letter from Lilia MacDonald to MacKay MacDonald- October 5, 1890 – George MacDonald
Collection. General Collection, Beinecke Rare Book and Manuscript Library, Yale University

In addition to us boarders, there were about two dozen day-scholars, and at recess the next day I had a successful fisticuff and was thereafter admitted to a small group who ruled the roost, especially among the boarding pupils. We carried large green slats from window shutters with *Sic Semper Tyrannis* carved on them. The meanest thing we did was to make smaller boys warm the seats of the outdoor privies on cold winter mornings, for our comfort. Arnoldus Vander Horst, of Charleston, was the ring leader in the initial Yankee-baiting and also the head of our little group."[74]

We see from his description that Ronald indeed had a huge responsibility as headmaster, as he was not only responsible for the care of his boys during school hours, but for the boarding students his responsibility was an around-the-clock job.

LOOKING NORTH ON SOUTH MAIN (NOW BILTMORE AVENUE), 1890'S.
ORIGINALLY PUBLISHED BY LINDSEY & BROWN,
LAND OF THE SKY, BEAUTIES OF WNC, CLASS A, ASHEVILLE & VICINITY, #104.
COURTESY, NC COLLECTIONS, PACK LIBRARY, ASHEVILLE, NC.

---

74   F. M. Huntington Wilson, *The Memoirs of An Ex-Diplomat*. (Boston: Bruce Humphries, Inc., 1945), p.27.

RONALD MACDONALD AS SKETCHED BY HIS WIFE
LOUISE VIRENDA BLANDY MACDONALD,
CIRCA 1880S. – FROM LOUISE'S SCRAPBOOK –
RF 1996B2838, RUSKIN FOUNDATION
RUSKIN LIBRARY, LANCASTER UNIVERSITY

RAVENSCROFT HIGH SCHOOL FOR BOYS — 1892
FROM "SOUVENIR OF ASHEVILLE OR THE SKY-LAND, 1892" BY
MRS. HARRIET ADAMS SAWYER, PAGE 83.
COURTESY D. H. RAMSEY LIBRARY, SPECIAL COLLECTIONS, UNC AT ASHEVILLE.

❖ Chapter 8 ❖
INNER LIFE

Ronald, though consumed with the overwhelming and demanding duties of teaching and managing the school, was suffering extreme grief over the loss of his beloved. In a letter from October 1890, after writing about the day to day duties he must attend to, he breaks down and confesses to his father:

> I have not thanked you for all your words of sweet comfort, nor have I attempted to tell you what my life is like – inside, I mean. It seems only a woof of desolation & warp of pain.[75] I would oh, so gladly die any minute, but with God's help & yours & Loo's last words I am slowly, very slowly, learning to live, I think.[76]

In another letter written to his father a month later Ronald wishes him a happy birthday, saying how much he loves his father and earnestly strives to follow his example:

> I almost wish I could be audacious enough to try to tell you what your life (the fact that you are, I mean) is to me. But it not only seems rather presumptuous, but I suppose that I should fail, even if I tried. But I wish the more that I was near you that I could let you see that my love and worship are very great. I suppose it is because I am so much behind what you would have me, that I think so much of this bodily presence. It may

75 The words woof and weft derive ultimately from the Old English word wefan, "to weave". It has given rise to the expression "woof and warp", meaning literally a fabric (the warp being the lengthwise threads, under and over which the side to side threads – the woof – are woven). The expression is used as a metaphor for the underlying structure on which something is built. – from Wikipedia-http://en.wikipedia.org/wiki/Weft

76 Letter from Ronald MacDonald to George MacDonald – October 9 & 18 & 19, 1890 – George MacDonald Collection. General Collection, Beinecke Rare Book and Manuscript Library, Yale University

be as you say unnecessary, yet it is only in the hope thereof, or some equivalent or superior contact, that I am able to live & love & keep from despair.[77]

Ronald writes near the end of the same letter a touching account of his deepening love for his baby Ozella, which reminds him of the love he had for his dear wife "Loo":

> Ozella flourishes & grows wiser too, in those things we think most of. Her great delight, now that we have a piano is to have me waltz with her intermittently. Most of the time she sings to herself. It is odd that I was just thinking the other day that I should never care to dance again, now Loo is gone, & since then it has become the regular thing for Ozella to have a dance with me before we go to bed. It makes me feel as though there were really three of us dancing. Perhaps it is so.[78]

Not surprisingly, holidays were dreadful for Ronald, as they brought on fresh reminders of his loss. That first Christmas of 1890, after Louise's passing, was perhaps the worst. On New Year's Day, 1891 he writes mournfully to his mother:

> I can't tell you how dreadful our little holiday has been to me. Death does indeed seem the sweetest possible thing to think of. I don't like work, & I hate leisure, and I am so awfully, fearfully, weary. I don't think anyone knows it here but Lily[…]. It is a sin and shame to be so unhappy as I am. I sin and I am ashamed – I am so small a thing alone. I can hardly pray for anything but the end. And yet there is much I desire-first and most to see you and & Father. I don't mope much dear, but I feel half dead inside with longing & a consequent & regular quiet that feels like despair. My whole mind is now filled with her & I can't get even a far off sense of her presence.[79]

---

77 Letter from Ronald MacDonald to George MacDonald – November 27, 1890 – George MacDonald Collection. General Collection, Beinecke Rare Book and Manuscript Library, Yale University

78 Ibid.

79 Letter from Ronald MacDonald to Louisa MacDonald- New Year's Day, 1891 – George MacDonald Collection. General Collection, Beinecke Rare Book and Manuscript Library, Yale University

George MacDonald felt deeply for Ronald and his loss. He publicly displayed his sympathy in February 1891 by dedicating his next novel, *There and Back* to Ronald. From his desk in Bordighera George penned a moving tribute:

> In the sure hope of everlasting brotherhood, I offer this book to Ronald MacDonald, my son and friend, my pupil, fellow-student, and fellow-workman.

Ravenscroft High School for Boys.

ASHEVILLE, N. C.

Ronald MacDonald, B. A. (Oxford), Head Master.

Ravenscroft High School for Boys will commence its sixth year, being the fourth under Mr. MacDonald's management, in September, 1892. The school owes its existence to the North Carolina Diocesan Conventions in 1886 and 1887, which aimed to supply the general demand for a Diocesan Classical School of a high character. The number of scholars is at present more than three times as great as the Head Master found in the school when it first came into his hands in the autumn of 1889. The work done has been satisfactory, the average marks showing a steady rise.

[Extract from the address of the Bishop of North Carolina at the Convention of the Diocese, 1891.]

"I was much cheered and encouraged by the increasing prosperity of Ravenscroft High School for Boys. Under the wise, able and judicious management of Mr. MacDonald, there has been a constant advance, and now the School has won for itself a very high reputation, and has secured the utmost confidence on the part of those whose sons have been enjoying its privileges. I feel quite sure that no more thorough and admirable school has ever been established in our State, and now its triumphant success seems fully assured. Parents may indeed consider it a high privilege to have their sons surrounded by influences so salutary and elevating, and where the training of mind, body and spirit are alike so constantly regarded.

"The school will need no further commendation to secure all the pupils who, under our present arrangements, can possibly be accommodated."

ADVERTISEMENT FROM "SOUVENIR OF ASHEVILLE OR THE SKY-LAND, 1892"
BY MRS. HARRIET ADAMS SAWYER, PAGE XI.
COURTESY D. H. RAMSEY LIBRARY, SPECIAL COLLECTIONS, UNC AT ASHEVILLE.

RAVENSCROFT HIGH SCHOOL WAS ONE OF ASHEVILLE'S LEADING EDUCATIONAL INSTITUTES IN EARLIER DAYS. IN THIS PHOTO, WHICH BELONGS TO GEORGE COLT, SOME OF THE STUDENTS ARE PICTURED WITH THE HEADMASTER, RONALD MACDONALD, WHOSE ENGLISH TRAINING SET THE EDUCATIONAL PATTERN FOR THE INSTITUTION. IDENTIFICATION OF THE BOYS REVEALS MANY WHO WERE TO BECOME COMMUNITY LEADERS. FROM L TO R: FRONT ROW, HAMILTON BIGELOW, P. C. COCKE, WALTER HATCH LEE, V. E. MCBEE JR., ARNOLD W. VANDERHORST, PRESTON PATTON, MCBEE HATCH AND C.C. MILLARD; SECOND ROW, MYNOT DAVIS, WALTON CHEESBOROUGH, CHARLES E. JONES, J. C. BURRAGE, H. K. MILLARD, RONALD MACDONALD, VERNON RAMSEUR AND WINTHROP CAMPBELL; BACK ROW, EUGENE HOLT, SILVO VON RUCK, J. E. CHEESBOROUGH, JAMES A. GWYN, PROF. P. S. PARKER, D. W. BISSEL, JAMES HYMAN, WALTER ERDMAN AND ERWIN HOLT.

PHOTO AND CAPTION FROM *ASHEVILLE CITIZEN TIMES*, JULY 1954

❖ CHAPTER 9 ❖

BELOVED HEADMASTER

Ronald kept a busy pace of teaching[80] and administrating, despite his lingering grief. In an undated letter, Lilia tells her sister Winifred:

> Ronald is just unpacking the last of his schoolbooks, & says now he will have 6 classes himself, 4 days in the week, & 7 on the 5th – (Saturdays is always a holiday hereabouts – a better thing for masters than boys) & he has to keep an eye on the whole school all the time – He has got them into beautiful order already, & they are quiet as mice.[81]

Ronald apparently was a fine teacher and headmaster. Lilia's letters often mentions what a fine teacher he is and the many compliments he received from satisfied parents. As an example of his excellent teaching skills, she tells about "little Charley":

> He is not nine yet, & cd. not write <u>at all</u> last spring. – When R[onald] had been teaching him 6 weeks he wrote home to his father without help. – I think it must have been the way R. taught him for he is not a clever child.[82]

---

80 One of Lilia's letters (December 15, 1890) was written on a discarded Report Card which contains a list of the subjects taught at Ravenscroft: Latin, Greek, Algebra, Arithmetic, English Literature, English grammar, History, Geography, Sacred Study, Composition, Reading, Declaration, Spelling, and Writing. The boys were also graded on the following character traits: Punctuality, Industry and Decorum.

81 Letter from Lilia MacDonald to Winifred MacDonald – December 1, 1890 – George MacDonald Collection. General Collection, Beinecke Rare Book and Manuscript Library, Yale University

82 Letter from Lilia MacDonald to Louisa MacDonald- October 15, 1890 – George MacDonald Collection. General Collection, Beinecke Rare Book and Manuscript Library, Yale University

Ronald was an excellent teacher and a beloved headmaster as well. Huntington Wilson,[83] a former Ravenscroft pupil, who later had a successful career in the US diplomatic corps, writes in his 1945 memoirs: "The school was run by Ronald Macdonald, a handsome man, the son of George Macdonald, the English novelist...."[84] Wilson also notes that, "The headmaster was crazy about riding and dressed well for the part; but he held himself so rigidly that he often took a spill."[85]

In one letter, Lilia proudly tells her mother how much the people love Ronald:

> Everyone we call on sings the praises of the school [...] I wish you cd. hear them – One mother says he is going to be the Dr. Arnold of N.C., another asks almost in terror if he is <u>certain</u> to stay here, another says her boys were never so happy & never worked so hard at school before. Another tells you he is so loved because he takes an interest out of school hours [...] When I returned the Pattons' call I had Captain Patton (R's chief enemy at first, you know) all to myself & he spake of R[onald] with enthusiasm.[86]

Ravenscroft after school hours took on a family-like atmosphere. Most evenings their little "family" consisted of Ronald, Lilia, Winnie, baby Ozella and Masters, Mr. D. W. Bissell and Mr. Parker, and frequent visitors, brothers, Herbert & Arthur Child.[87] Mr. Bissell, a Yale graduate, was the first professor hired to assist Ronald with the teaching. One former student described Master Bissell as "small and dapper...."[88] Mr. Parker, was a recent Harvard graduate, who had been hired not long after Lilia's arrival. Many evenings it seemed, they all would sit in the drawing room around the table and play a card game of "whist." Lilia and Ronald frequently allude to these evening sessions.

83 Francis Mairs Huntington Wilson, Ravenscroft pupil 1889-1891.

84 F. M. Huntington Wilson, The Memoirs of An Ex-Diplomat. (Boston: Bruce Humphries, Inc., 1945), p.27.

85 Ibid.

86 Letter from Lilia MacDonald to Louisa MacDonald – November 5, 1890 – George MacDonald Collection. General Collection, Beinecke Rare Book and Manuscript Library, Yale University

87 The 1890 Asheville City Directory lists: Herbert Child, bds. Van Gilder House; Arthur Steele Child, architect and draftsman, bds. Van Gilder House.

88 F. M. Huntington Wilson, The Memoirs of An Ex-Diplomat. (Boston: Bruce Humphries, Inc., 1945), p.27.

But sometimes, Lilia gives us a sense of their playful camaraderie:

> – The whist players are expressing themselves with great
> freedom. "I hate Parker worse than death," says Mr. Bissell in
> his quiet way – "You will find Bissell, that more can be done
> with some natures by kindness than by severity," says R[onald]
> with the eternal pipe in his mouth. It is a mercy that I can
> stand 'baccy better than when I was young, as we sit nightly
> in a cloud.[89]

They would often tease and taunt each other like brothers and
sisters. Lilia relates to her sister Winifred of one amusing incident:

> [...] Mr. Bissell & headmaster [Ronald], who are making out
> the monthly reports[...] Ozella may be heard in the distance
> crooning a cheerful song. I am writing to my mother at a side
> table waiting until the gentleman have done their pipes and
> classifications & are ready for me to make out the results-
> Suddenly the window opens – Winnie B.'s head pops in
> interrupting, "Bush is not below 80 in anything – Vanderhorst
> is 90 in grammar – that boy does very well with me[...] etc."
> with the solemn – "Lily, that child [Ozella] has just said yes
> distinctly with the s. I asked her if she was cosy and she said
> yes just as you or I wd." We are all gratified, but not so thrilled
> as Winnie, whose need for stirring incident in life can be fed at
> very small flames. R. & I grunt our satisfaction, & Mr. Bissell
> says very seriously, "Are you sure you are not doing very wrong
> to teach her to say yes, when perhaps she ought to be saying
> no?" The window is banged indignantly, W[innie] disappears
> & R. says, "Is it Hood who speaks of Shutting the door with a
> wooden damn?[90]

---

89 Letter from Lilia MacDonald to Winifred MacDonald – undated – George MacDonald
Collection. General Collection, Beinecke Rare Book and Manuscript Library, Yale University

90 Letter from Lilia MacDonald to Winifred MacDonald – undated – George MacDonald
Collection. General Collection, Beinecke Rare Book and Manuscript Library, Yale University

LOUISE'S GRAVESITE (FOREGROUND) WITH A VIEW TO THE SOUTHWEST.
IN 1890, ONE COULD SEE DOWN TO THE RIVER AND
BEYOND TO THE DISTANT MOUNTAINS.

LOUISE BLANDY MACDONALD'S GRAVE MARKER

CHAPTER 10

LIFE IN ASHEVILLE

Lilia and Ronald's letters often tell of their adventures away from the school as well. Lilia relates an interesting story of an incident on a visit to the dentist:

> I went with Winnie to the dentist – She was naturally very nervous at anyone but her father touching her mouth, so I said some little thing @ it-He [the dentist] asked her name, & then said it was a name he knew as he had studied under a Dr. Blandy of Charleston (?) & had worked for his father-in-law, Dr. Harris – You may imagine this delighted Winnie! He spoke of her beautiful mother & of all the family. Afterwd. Winnie told me what I shd. have liked to know before, that her grandfather wrote the book[91] that is <u>the</u> authority in the S[outhern] States on Dental Surgery & her father still gets £100 from the publishers for its sale & there is a public statue to him, Dr. Harris, in the principal square as well – is it Charleston or Baltimore? – the latter I think.[92]

In another letter, Lilia writes with sweetness of a three-quarter of a mile journey across town to visit Louise's grave at "Riverside Cemetery":

> Winnie & I went to church in the morning & then walked

---

91 *The Dental Art, a Practical Treatise on Dental Surgery.* by Chapin Aaron Harris, 1839. Armstrong & Berry: Baltimore. This tome went through numerous editions – including a reprint as recent as 1979.

92 Letter from Lilia MacDonald to Winifred MacDonald – December 1, 1890 – George MacDonald Collection. General Collection, Beinecke Rare Book and Manuscript Library, Yale University

down to the cemetery – I had not been before – R. was always saying he wd. take me, but he just hates walking, & I thought it better to go when W. asked me. – It is a lovely walk & the cemetery itself is a beautiful spot & it is very nicely kept! Our dear one's long green grave is under a tree with the most lovely view of a rather distant broad river at the feet, with a horizon of blue hills & just now, gorgeous colouring of trees on the river. W. & I had the greatest trouble to get any flowers. In despair, we broke off boughs of crimson leaves as we went along, & at last found a nigress to sell us some of the Chrysanthemums in her garden.[93]

Lilia's descriptions of Asheville and its surroundings are numerous and often critical. Of course she's comparing it to her experience of living in the metropolis of London and the lush Mediterranean Riviera of Italy. Also Asheville was in the midst of a "boom," with the recent coming of the railroad, and the city was scrambling to update its infrastructure to catch up with the rising population. Perhaps her best observations are those she puts in a long letter to her brother MacKay:

You cannot conceive what awful state the roads are in – I, in my narrow European experience had no idea you cd. apply the word road to such lengths of holes & hillocks of red mud or red dust, according to the weather…. And this place calls itself a City – Ronald says he had quite a trouble with Winnie when she first came because she would be so heedless as to talk of the <u>village</u> – It is a nice sized village – & the third largest City in N.C. – With all this muss and muddle the trams go by electricity[94] & up to 12:00 nights. There is a beautiful little opera house. The bank – a hideous <u>castellated</u> building is filled with plate glass & brass, as are many of the shops – (but the plate glass & the brass are not kept clean). There are many other modern improvements, but I forget what they are. – Vanderbilt- the youngest has bought a huge amount of miles of an estate with a private railway to it, outside the town. – They say there are some pretty gardens round the houses outside the town, but so far I've only seen one & the rest are down-trodden patches of <u>field grass</u> with perhaps in the middle a miserable squirt

93 Letter from Lilia MacDonald to Louisa MacDonald – October 29, 1890 – George MacDonald Collection. General Collection, Beinecke Rare Book and Manuscript Library, Yale University

94 Asheville's "electric trains," or trolleys, which began operation in 1889 were the first in the U.S.

representing I presume a fountain. The houses are either wood or a peculiarly hideous shade of deep red brick. Many of the wood houses are painted drab-both styles singularly unadapted to the brilliant light & the soft intense blues of the hills (called mountains here) & the sky. The effect is much the same that it wd. be to have red brick on the Riviera. & I think white houses if they can't have stone ones wd. be a most distinct improvement.[95]

LOOKING WEST DOWN PATTON AVENUE FROM SQUARE, ASHEVILLE, NC, C. 1890'S.
NOTICE "ELECTRIC TRAIN" IN BACKGROUND.

COURTESY NC COLLECTION, PACK LIBRARY, ASHEVILLE, NC.

Lilia's observations of the state of the roads and difficulties in navigating one's way through the Asheville streets was confirmed by a former Asheville resident and Ravenscroft student, who writes: "Everyone rode horseback down there at that time. In fact, at wet seasons it was the only way to get about. Wagons would sink up to the hubs in the clay soup that some of the roads became."[96]

Ronald and Louise were communicants at Trinity Episcopal Church which was not only just outside the gate of the Ravenscroft grounds, but was the sponsoring church of the school. Therefore the

95 Letter from Lilia MacDonald to MacKay MacDonald – October 5, 1890 – George MacDonald Collection. General Collection, Beinecke Rare Book and Manuscript Library, Yale University

96 F. M. Huntington Wilson, *The Memoirs of An Ex-Diplomat*. (Boston: Bruce Humphries, Inc., 1945), p.27.

boy's were required to attend as well. The Rev. Jarvis Buxton, the rector of the church for many years, lived on "Buxton Hill" next to Schoenberger Hall, just down the road from Ravenscroft. Having been the founder of Ravenscroft in the 1850s, Rev. Buxton was elderly and semi-retired, and by Ronald's time would only occasionally preach at the church. He did perform Louise's funeral. Lilia's letters often refer to the church services they attended at Trinity while she was at Ravenscroft. She mentions various preachers such as Rev. Buxton, Rev. D. H. Buel (who ran the Seminary of Ravenscroft in Schoenberger Hall), Rev. McNeely Dubose, and a Rev. Owen (a visiting Englishman, who Lilia did not care for). Lilia writes home of her first service after arriving in Asheville:

> We went to church in solemn file yesterday – The service is rather nicely done, & the organ good – though American refinement has made alterations that jar a good deal on the English mind & ear.[97]

INTERIOR OF TRINITY EPISCOPAL CHURCH, ASHEVILLE NC C. 1890

97 Letter from Lilia MacDonald to Winifred MacDonald – September 21, 1890 – George MacDonald Collection. General Collection, Beinecke Rare Book and Manuscript Library, Yale University

In a later letter, Lilia again mentions the difference of the American wording of the litany from the English. And Ronald, being the consummate historian, gives her an explanation for the difference:

> They give a nice communion here – the words are a little altered but not much. – Ronald says that is because we behaved very badly after the Revolution & refused to consecrate American bishops – & a Scotch Bishop did it & that had an effect on the wording of the service.[98]

Perhaps the kindest description Lilia gives is her description of the funeral service for Rev. D. H. Buel's wife. Rev. Buel had for years run the theological training division of Ravenscroft but by the time of his wife's death, Lilia tells us, he was too feeble to accompany his wife's body to her burial in New York. But the funeral service was held at Trinity Church. Lily reports: "The service was very nicely given, & old Dr. Buxton read the lesson magnificently – He had a very impressive port & delivery, & is an ecclesiastic all over – I was very glad I went...."[99]

TRINITY EPISCOPAL CHURCH, ASHEVILLE NC C. 1890S

98 Letter from Lilia MacDonald to Louisa MacDonald – October 29, 1890 – George MacDonald Collection. General Collection, Beinecke Rare Book and Manuscript Library, Yale University

99 Letter from Lilia MacDonald to Louisa MacDonald – February 6, 1891 – George MacDonald Collection. General Collection, Beinecke Rare Book and Manuscript Library, Yale University

Being the son of a famous and beloved author had its perks – such as being well liked just for being "George MacDonald's son." Lilia often mentions in her letters of encounters with people who tell her how much they love her father. In a letter to her mother, after telling her how excited the boys were that Ronald had taught them bookbinding, she says:

> Bush (one of the boys) bound a lot of his own books at home in the holidays he says. He is such a nice boy, very quiet- Mr. Parker says his grandmother is a most charming old Phila. lady, who says she loves Ronald already because he is his father's son, on whose books she <u>was brought up</u> – that tickled me – I wonder how old she is.[100]

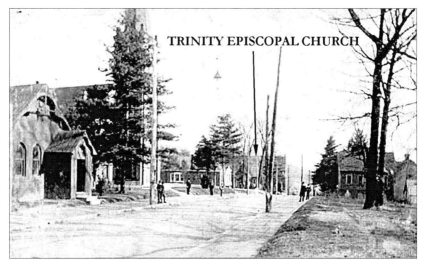

LOOKING DOWN CHURCH STREET
COURTESY NC COLLECTIONS, PACK LIBRARY, ASHEVILLE, NC

---

100 Letter from Lilia MacDonald to Louisa MacDonald – January 22, 1891 – George MacDonald Collection. General Collection, Beinecke Rare Book and Manuscript Library, Yale University

❖ Chapter 11 ❖

LILIA GOES HOME

By March of 1891 Lilia had been in Asheville for over eight months and with things seeming to be running smoothly for Ronald and the school, Ronald begins to talk of Lilia's leaving. He writes to his mother:

> How selfish I feel in keeping Lily all this while. I cannot tell you, and indeed I ought now to be able to do without & can at a moment's notice. What she has been to me, nobody could say, nor what she has been to everybody in the house.[101]

And yet a week later, Lilia writes of Ronald's fatigue and weariness:

> Ronald finds it, – I think, more & more of a struggle to keep on – He needs a change dreadfully, & if there was anywhere reasonably near he cd. go to, I think he could be persuaded to get away for Easter. But there isn't – & the jog trot sameness of the days here, wh[ich] is so resting and even refreshing to me, is full of little edges & notches & thorns to him, which makes it very, very wearing, & teaching tires him so much more than it used (to).[102]

Lilia and Ronald both agree that it is time for her to leave, yet they know that Ronald will need someone to take her place as matron. Also Winnie is beginning to talk of going back home as well, which seems to be welcomed by Ronald. Lilia writes to her mother about the

---

101 Letter from Ronald MacDonald to Louisa MacDonald – March 8, 1891 – George MacDonald Collection. General Collection, Beinecke Rare Book and Manuscript Library, Yale University

102 Letter from Lilia MacDonald to Louisa MacDonald – March 19, 1891- George MacDonald Collection. General Collection, Beinecke Rare Book and Manuscript Library, Yale University

situation:

> He [Ronald] says it is imperative that I sh. see @ getting a
> berth, but I cannot convince him to see he cd. go, nor can I
> get him to say I may write & ask Jessie when she cd. come
> out. To leave him alone here, wd. half kill him, I am sure,
> especially in vacation, with nothing he must do every day. – I
> am glad W[innie] seems quite decided always on departing,
> when the summer vacation comes, as she gets more & more
> on R's nerves. – & the more resolutions she makes @ seeing
> to domestic matters, the less she seems to carry them out. – I
> suppose she & I will go together."[103]

Interestingly to the public, who were not privy to the behind-
the-scenes emotional and personal trials of their beloved headmaster,
things seemed to be progressing quite nicely. In fact that Spring (1891)
the Bishop of the North Carolina Episcopal Church reports in a
promotional advertisement in a popular tourist periodical:

> Ravenscroft High School for Boys will commence its fifth
> year, being the third under Mr. MacDonald's management,
> on September 16, 1891. The school owes its existence to the
> North Carolina Diocesan Conventions in 1886 and 1887,
> which aimed to supply the general demand for a Diocesan
> classical school of a high character. The session of 1890-91
> has been highly encouraging to those engaged in the work of
> this school. The numbers have been higher than ever before,
> and the finances far more satisfactory than in previous years.
> The number of scholars is at present three times as great as the
> head master found in the school when it first came into his
> hands in the autumn of 1889. The course set down in the last
> prospectus has been adhered to with very slight modification.
> The work done has been satisfactory, the average marks
> showing a steady rise. The nucleus of a school library has been
> formed, the books being chosen by the committee, in which
> the head master has the right of veto as well as the privilege of
> suggestion. The intention is to get, without any undue pressure,
> a sound selection of healthy books into the school and into the
> favor of the scholars. The climate of Asheville affords excellent
> opportunity for spending much time in the open air. This

---

103 Ibid.

fact is worthy of attention on the part of parents whose sons need a mild and bracing atmosphere. The school buildings are situated on high and extensive grounds, the property of the Diocese, in the city of Asheville, and thus afford the advantages of perfect: healthfulness, charming scenery, and ample grounds for sports.[104]

Lilia and Winnie finally did return to England in the Spring of 1891, following the end of the school term. Lilia went back home to England, mainly to nurse her dear friend Eva Pym, who was dying of tuberculosis. Sadly, Lilia, the ever-sacrificing servant made her final sacrifice for her friend – for she soon contracted the deadly disease herself and within seven months of leaving Ravenscroft she was dead.

George MacDonald, who experienced the early deaths of three of his siblings and four of his grown children, referred to tuberculosis as "the family attendant." But to him and indeed to all the family, the death of Lilia was almost too much to bear. Perhaps the most quoted of George MacDonald's letters is the one that he had written to Lilia on the occasion of her 39th birthday in January 1891, just nine months before her passing, while she was at Ravenscroft.

> I could say so much to you, and yet I am constantly surrounded by a sort of cactus-hedge that seems to make adequate utterance impossible. It is so much easier to write romances where you cannot easily lie, than to say the commonest things where you may go wrong any moment. [...]I can only tell you I love you with true heart fervently, and love you far more because you are God's child than because you are mine. I don't thank you for coming to us, for you could not help it, but the whole universe is "tented" with love, and you hold one of the corners of the great love-canopy for your mother and me. I don't think I am very ambitious, except the strong desire "to go where I am" be ambition; and I know I take small satisfaction in looking on my past; but I do live expecting great things in the life that is ripening for me and all mine – when we shall all have the universe for our own, and be good merry helpful children in the great house of our Father. I think then we shall be able to pass into and through each other's very souls as we please,

---

104 Chapin, George H. *Health Resorts of the South: containing numerous engravings descriptive of the most desirable resorts of the southern states.* 1892.

knowing each other's thought and being, along with our own, and so being like God. When we are all just as loving and unselfish as Jesus; when like him, our one thought of delight is that God is, and is what he is; when the fact that a being is just another person from ourselves is enough to make that being precious – then darling, you and I all will have the grand liberty wherewith Christ makes free-opening his hand to send us out like white doves to range the Universe.

Have I now shown that the attempt to speak what I mean is the same kind of failure that walking is – a mere, constantly recurring recovery from falling? [...]

I have still one great poem in my mind, but it will never be written, I think, except we have a fortune left us, so that I need not write any more stories of which I am beginning to be tired.

My dear love to Ronald. I could not bear you to leave him any more could yourself. Tell him from me that Novalis says: "This world is not a dream, but it may, and perhaps ought to become one." Anyhow it will pass – to make way for the world God has hidden in our hearts.

Darling, I wish you life eternal. I daresay the birthdays will still be sparks in its glory. May I see the mould out of which you came. [105]

---

105 Glenn Edward Sadler, _An Expression of Character: The Letters of George MacDonald._ (Grand Rapids, MI: Wm. B Eerdmmans Publishing, 1994), pp. 343-44.

LILIA SCOTT MACDONALD
PHOTOGRAPH BY CHARLES DODGSON
AKA LEWIS CARROLL
COURTESY BEINECKE LIBRARY, YALE UNIVERSITY

RONALD WROTE TO HIS SISTER WINIFRED IN 1892 AFTER THE DEATH OF THEIR
SISTER LILIA. RONALD AND WINNIE ARE STANDING NEXT TO ONE ANOTHER
ON THE FAR RIGHT. THIS PHOTOGRAPH (CIRCA 1877) IS FROM LILIA'S PHOTO
ALBUM COURTESY OF THE BEINECKE LIBRARY AT YALE UNIVERSITY.

WINNIE WAS CLOSEST IN AGE TO RONALD AND, ALONG WITH LILIA, OFTEN ASSUMED THE
ROLE OF FAMILY CARETAKER. SHE HELPED WITH THE TYPING OF THREE LILITH MANUSCRIPTS
AND HAD THE FORESIGHT, AFTER IT'S PUBLICATION IN 1895, TO ASK HER FATHER FOR ALL
THE MANUSCRIPTS. SHE LOOKED AFTER HER PARENTS DURING THE 1890S UNTIL, AT AGE
40, SHE MARRIED C. EDWARD TROUP IN 1898. AFTER HER SISTER, GRACE, WAS MARRIED IN
1904, GEORGE CAME TO LIVE WITH WINNIE AND EDWARD FOR THE LAST NINE MONTHS OF HIS
LIFE. WINNIE PUBLISHED HER MOTHER'S DRAMATIZED PILGRIM'S PROGRESS II WITH OXFORD
UNIVERSITY PRESS IN 1925 AND IN 1946, AS THE LAST SURVIVING SIBLING AT THE AGE OF 88,
SHE PRESENTED THE EIGHT WORKING DRAFTS OF LILITH TO THE BRITISH MUSEUM. THEY ARE
CURRENTLY HOUSED AT THE BRITISH LIBRARY.

❖ Chapter 12 ❖
CARRYING ON

Ronald, of course, keenly felt the loss of his beloved sister, especially considering that it had been barely a year since Louise's passing. Two months after Lilia's passing, Ronald writes a sympathy letter to his sister Winnie. Though he sends his sympathies, one can tell that Lilia's death has only served to uncover the still festering pangs of grief over his dear wife's death:

> My heart is very sore for you all in the terrible loneliness you must feel without Lily. But indeed you must have a comfort I never have – you must all be able, unless you have changed a great deal, to bring her back among you by sweet talk of her – a kind of talk, it seems to me, which is one of the highest privileges of common affection. I think I should be measurably happier among a set of people who had known Louise as your house, & much of your neighborhood knew and prized Lilia. In addition to the joys of hope & memory which such outspoken sympathy cherishes, it undoubtedly helps a man to face instead of avoid his grief. Of course I have here several persons to whom I can speak of her, or Lily. But conversation on either of course cannot spring up, & cheer one unexpectedly with the fresh & vivid sense of eternity which he so sadly needs.[106]

Ronald plodded on with his work at Ravenscroft for the next few years, feeling duty bound to work out his five-year contract. Jessie

---

106 Letter from Ronald MacDonald to Winifred MacDonald – Saturday, January 16, 1892 – George MacDonald Collection. General Collection, Beinecke Rare Book and Manuscript Library, Yale University

Sharman, Louisa MacDonald's elderly cousin, came to replace Lilia. Only a few letters remain of correspondence from those two years, as Lilia had been the prolific letter writer. There are a few from Jessie and even fewer from Ronald. The few that do remain give us the impression that the work was carrying on just as it had when Louise and Lilia were there, only certainly with less enthusiasm and cheer. Like Lilia's letters, cousin Jessie's are descriptive of life at Ravenscroft, though her observations are more "matronly" than Lilia's. In a rather lengthy letter, she tells of the new masters, who she says, are rather selfish and uncaring, unlike Mr. Bissell and Mr. Parker whom she holds in high esteem. In the same letter, she reveals that Ronald had finally found something to occupy his mind during those difficult days of holiday vacation:

> We gave two plays on January 4th & 5th in the evening & had invited about 25 people each night, as only half of them could get here, we had to repeat the performance the following week in the afternoon, and had such a crowd, just two days before the boy's returned. – such a rush it made, as we had turned their common room into a theatre & used all their dormitory curtains[107] for the stage. – The plays were "The Chimney Corner" & "Apples". – The preparations & having two nice girls in & out made the holidays very pleasant. The 2 Masters, 2 boys, Ronald & I took the other parts. Ronald was splendid as an old man...[108]

Little Ozella was becoming very popular and was now speaking quite well. Jessie writes that Ozella received a "table full" of presents for Christmas. The list included dolls, gloves "with fur tops", a pair of red shoes, money, a silver salt cellar, and "many books – some of these from the Meigs."[109] Ozella apparently created a bit of a stir, as Jessie writes: "She startled one or two people by telling them she had her presents on

---

107 F.M. Huntington Wilson in his *Memoirs of An Ex-Diplomat* tells us that the boarding students at Ravenscroft were housed "in a dormitory with cubicles curtained off." These cubicle curtains, as well as the window curtains, were no doubt the ones used for these dramatic productions.

108 Letter from Janet Sharman to Winfred MacDonald – January 25, 1892 – George MacDonald Collection. General Collection, Beinecke Rare Book and Manuscript Library, Yale University

109 Dr. & Mrs. John Meigs – then Headmaster of Hill School, Pottstown, PA. Ronald became lifelong friends of the Meigs family. In 1906 Ronald dedicated his novel, *Sea Maid* to: "John Meigs, Ph. D., from whose goodness and humor if this story draw smile and laugh it is well it was written".

"Our Heavenly Father's Son's birthday" – as everyone here teaches their children to expect their presents from Santa Claus."[110] In the same letter Jessie, who like Lilia sees it as her job to report to the family how Ronald is doing, even though she writes, "you know how sensitive he is about being made a subject of conversation"[111] tells us anyway:

> He is a little happier than he was, tho' he grieves terribly at times, & I think feels even more than ever how much he wants Louise, to help him through all the trials & difficulties that must arise from time to time in connection with his work here. – He seems now & then to be so completely overwhelmed with the feeling that there is no object to work for, it is very dreary for him poor fellow & tho' Ozella is a great joy, there is always mixed with that the feeling that the Mother is not here to share it.[112]

The death of Virenda and Lilia were not only difficult for Ronald, but also for his aging father, George MacDonald, whose own lifetime of suffering was beginning to tire him. But George's faith in a transcendent loving God, continued to give him hope. In the Spring of 1892, George writes to his first cousin Helen:

> I think we feel – Louisa and I at least – as if we were getting ready to go. The world is very different since Lily went, and we shall be glad when our time comes to go after our children. I hope and trust more and more as I grow older. The boys are no anxiety to us – except that Ronald suffers much. But he is very brave and diligent, and has the quaintest darling of a child – odd and pretty like her name, Ozella.[113]

Ronald does seem at least to be able to get away from his work a little more often now. In fact he takes one entire letter to his sister Winfred to relate an adventurous outing he undertook to a nearby town. He writes:

> I had meant for some time to write you an account of our little journey in the hills [...] – Well, our friend, Mr. Child, brother

---

110 Ibid.

111 Ibid.

112 Ibid.

113 Letter from George MacDonald to Helen McKay Powell, April 16, 1892. – Glenn Edward Sadler, *An Expression of Character: The Letters of George MacDonald*. (Grand Rapids, MI: Wm. B Eerdmmans Publishing, 1994), pp. 349-50.

of him who lived here for a time, took Jessie & Ozella in a two horse buggy, with two wretched mustang ponies to draw them. My own pretty black horse had had ten days rest for a strained shoulder & the vet told me he was fit to travel. Our first stage was 32 miles to the chief town of the next county, far from railways & telegraphs. When we had got some way I found he went dead lame on a trot, but walked fairly well & without pain. I got an old farmer to take my card with directions to my nigger boy Josiah to drive out Jessie's brown cob to Brevard, county town above mentioned, (really a tiny village). After getting wet to the skin we dined & I changed clothes at a jolly farm house (jolly for America-nothing like an English one). The carriage then started again & I went off on my slow equine walk to try to beg, borrow, or hire a farm horse to take me to Brevard, another 16 miles. I failed utterly and added two miles to my woes, & the result was that I got into the town about 11 at night after walking slowly, sometimes on my own, sometimes on my nag's feet, over what you would think vile roads, tho' I thought them good, for many hours in pitch darkness, for eighteen miles. That makes 34 miles, of which I don't think I trotted two. I was more tired than if I had galloped the whole way. For the last part I had to wake up, I think, four sleeping households, to ask the way & met with nothing but kindness everywhere, except at a cursed little conventicle. Here seeing lights and people sitting, & hearing a voice & not knowing their pious engagements, I pulled up & shouted civil inquiries. A young man & a girl saw me & heard me & were too damned pious to get up for a minute. I rode on & if I didn't curse them, it wasn't their fault. This is sectarian Christianity as she is practiced.

Well the inn at Brevard wasn't bad in spite of slightly stinking cookery; the village cheerful & sunny in spite of the perpetual no beer curse, the weather not too hot, & the country lovely. Saturday & Sunday I stayed there with Ozella, while Mr. C. took Jessie & his beastly broncos to a large hotel[114] at the top of a large mountain with a large view. Hill called Caesar's head because it has a rock like the head of a dog & somebody once

---

114 Caesar's Head Hotel – Col. Hagood operated Caesars Head hotel on the Jones Gap Road that ran from Greenville, South Carolina to Asheville, North Carolina.-*http://www.carolinaliving.com/ visiting/history_mountains.asp.*

had a dog called Caesar. See the point? I don't. On Sunday evening they came back from the Hotel of the Imperial Dog, and while Jonah & the cob & the two-wheel cart had arrived from Asheville on Saturday night, I mounted Jessie's horse & we started on our next stage, 34 miles I think. But oh how I wish I could give you an idea of the Hotel at Brevard, of all the people I saw there, of the character of each horse and pony, of Mr. C. & of the desperately sordid difference of every thing from what you know.[115]

CAESAR'S HEAD C. 1890S

Although there is no correspondence to validate it, we know from other sources that Ronald worked out his contract at Ravenscroft and in 1894 he moved back to England. The last mention of Ronald in connection with the school is found in an article from *The Daily Citizen* in 1895 which reports:

115 Letter from Ronald MacDonald to Winifred MacDonald – August 18, 1892 – George MacDonald Collection. General Collection, Beinecke Rare Book and Manuscript Library, Yale University

> Ravenscroft High School for Boys was established in 1850 and has had various vicissitudes owing to constant change of management. In spite of this great disadvantage, however, it has always been able to obtain people. Under the management of Mr. Ronald MacDonald it attained considerable success. That gentleman abandoning it suddenly in the Fall of '94 it was given in charge of Mr. Toynbee Wight, who at present has a satisfactory number of people to whom he is imparting a thorough English and classical education.[116]

That short article is very poignant for two reasons. First, it was obvious that Ronald had hidden his grief so well that people would describe his leaving, fours years after his wife's death, as "abandoning it suddenly." Second, the article was adjacent to a large collage of photographs of "Asheville Public School Buildings." The rise of the free public school system in the US, and especially in Asheville where four pubic schools were established from 1888-1895, was the cause of the demise of the Ravenscroft School which ceased to exist by the end of the 1890s. That Ronald foresaw the trend is shown in a 1891 letter from Lilia to her mother:

> R's opinion & experience is quite adverse to belief in the success of an Englishman out here as schoolmaster. Free public schools have lowered the price of education all over the country, & that produces an inferior article of master in the average one, & the parents are content with him, or if not, send their boys to the public (in the sense of our board) schools.[117]

---

116 Women's Edition *The Daily Citizen*. – Thanksgiving Day, 1895 – front page. – Microfilm: Pack Library, Asheville, NC.

117 Letter from Lilia MacDonald to Louisa MacDonald – Tuesday, February 17, 1891 – George MacDonald Collection. General Collection, Beinecke Rare Book and Manuscript Library, Yale University

CHAPTER 13

EPILOGUE

Upon his return to England, Ronald gave up teaching and pursued a career in the theatre as an actor, playwright, and producer. After a few minor roles, Ronald had his "big break" in 1896, when he collaborated on a play with H. A. Saintsbury, titled "The Eleventh Hour." Ronald was not only co-producer, but also was one of the actors, taking the leading role of "Lord Edgbaston." The play toured England for two years. One of his co-actors was a young actress, Constance Robertson, whom he married in 1897. They had two children, Philip and Mary.

Though I have no indication if Ozella ever married, I know that she lived to the age of 29, dying in 1918.

Ronald later, following in the footsteps of his father, became a novelist. He even produced a silent movie, *Gambier's Advocate* in 1915, based on one of his novels by the same name. Ronald's son Philip also became a writer[118], mostly of mystery novels, the first two being co-authored with his father, using a pseudonym. In 1931, after marrying F. Ruth Howard,[119] Philip moved from England to Hollywood and

---

118 G. K. Chesterton honored George MacDonald, by writing the introduction to Greville MacDonald's biography in 1924. But Philip returned a compliment to Chesterton in his most acclaimed 1938 suspense novel, *Warrant for X*. The opening sentence reads: "The fact that Sheldon Garrett was an American makes it comprehensible that, although a widely traveled and widely read person, it was not until his thirty-fourth birthday that he made acquaintance with the work of Mr. G. K. Chesterton." Later, Garret purchases a copy of Chesterton's *The Napoleon of Notting Hill*, "perhaps the best of all Mr. Chesterton's good work." Then, while searching for places mentioned in the novel he is "led, as it were, by Chance and Chesterton." As a short article in *Gilbert Magazine* remarks of the book's plot: "What he finds sets the stage for his own adventures." ("An Accomplished Gentleman: Phillip MacDonald, (1900-1980)," by David Beresford, *Gilbert Magazine*. Volume 12, Number 6, May/April 2009).

119 All the biographies (books, articles & websites) that I have found of Philip talk of his marriage to F. Ruth Howard in 1931, however my research through the family letters and genealogical sources show that he first married Mona Fairlie Ventris, in 1925, with whom he had a daughter, Caryl

became a noted screenwriter.[120] Ronald died on July 13, 1933, in Earls Court, London.[121]

Ronald's seven year sojourn in America is a story that needed to be told, as it was not only largely untold before now, but also it is the type of seemingly isolated story that really combines with other stories to make up the fabric of "history." What a sad time it was for Ronald with the loss of his beloved wife, Louise. His subsequent grief and loneliness was exacerbated by being exiled far from his family and friends. Yet in the end, he returned to England and began a new life, by remarrying and starting a new family and a new career. His legacy continued through his son, Philip.

The history of the Ravenscroft High School for Boys, largely untold, also takes on new significance through the story of its headmaster and his family. The Ravenscroft building[122] still stands in downtown Asheville, not only as the oldest extant structure in the city, but now as a symbol and reminder of the lives of the many boys and teachers who studied, taught, and lived within its walls.

MacDonald, born in 1926. He was married to Mona, I know at least until October 1930, because Ronald wrote a letter from Philip & Mona's house, Stanborough Cottage, Hatfield, Hertshire, England on October 21, 1930. Interestingly, Mona & Caryl appear on a list of "alien passengers" on board the "Drechtyke" sailing from London to San Francisco, CA on August 14, 1934. Next to each of their names is stamped: "Admitted Sec 6 for Perm. Res."

120 See Wikipedia- http://en.wikipedia.org/wiki/Philip MacDonald

121 News of Ronald's death was reported the same day in the *New York Times*:

RONALD MACDONALD – NOVELIST, DEAD, 72

Was Also Dramatist – He had Returned to England After Teaching in U.S.

Wireless to the New York Times

LONDON, July 13 – Ronald MacDonald, novelist and dramatist, died here today at the age of 72. After leaving Oxford in 1885, he was a schoolmaster in the United States until 1894, when he returned to England and began his literary career.

Mr. MacDonald was the second son of George MacDonald, LL, D. He married twice. His first wife was Louise Blandy; his second Constance Robertson, daughter of the late Captain Henry Robertson of the First Life Guards. By his second marriage he had a son and daughter.

Among his novels are *The Sword of the King*, *The Red Herring* and *Green Handkerchief*. Under the pseudonym of Oliver Fleming he wrote, in collaboration with his son, Philip, *Ambrotox and Limping Dick* and *The Spandau Quid*.

122 Now on the National Register of Historic Places.

Modern Day Ravenscroft

Top: Ronald's Study

Middle: The Drawing room, from which many letters were written and cards played.

Bottom: Ravenscroft exterior

Ronald & Louise Virenda MacDonald
Significant Dates

1860 • October 27 - Ronald MacDonald is born at Tudor Lodge, Albert Street, London, England.

1861 • Louise Virenda Blandy is born in Baltimore, Maryland to Dr. Alfred A. & Ozillah Blandy.

1885 • Ronald graduates from Oxford with a BA in History.

1887 • April 27 - Ronald MacDonald & Louise Blandy become engaged to be married.

• September 2 - In Bar Harbor, Maine tutoring.

• September 26 - Begins his first term at Hill School, Pottstown, Pennsylvania.

• Winter - Louise "wintering" with the MacDonalds at Casa Coraggio, Bordighera, Italy.

1888 • Spring - Ronald finishes second term at Hill School and returns to England.

• July 7 - Ronald & Louise are married in Hendon, Greater London, England.

• Summer - Ronald & Louise spend time at the seaside town of Littlehampton, England.

• September - Ronald & Louise go back to Hill School to begin Fall Term.

• November - Louise writes a letter to Winifred MacDonald from Hill School.

1889 • Jan. - May- Ronald & Louise spend a second term at Hill School.

• May - Ronald contemplates starting his own school in Alabama.

- Possible time of birth of daughter - Ozella Louise MacDonald in Pottstown, Pa.
- Ronald learns of position at Ravenscroft and investigates.
- August - mid-September Ronald & Louise return for a visit to England, possibly to register Ozella's birth.
- September 18 - Ronald begins as headmaster of Ravenscroft High School for Boys, Asheville, NC.

1890
- January 2 - Easter term begins at Ravenscroft.
- June - It becomes evident the Louise is gravely ill.
- July 9 - Varina "Winnie" Blandy, arrives at Ravenscroft.
- August 27 - Louise Virenda Blandy MacDonald dies at Ravenscroft.
- August 28 - Louise is buried in the Riverside Cemetery, Asheville, with Rev. Jarvis Buxton, officiating.
- September 12 - Lilia arrives at Ravenscroft.
- late September - Fall term begins at Ravenscroft.

1891
- April - Lilia and Winnie both return to England.
- Fall - Jessie Sharman comes to Ravenscroft as Lilia & Winnie's replacement.
- November 22 - Lilia Scott MacDonald dies at Bordighera, Italy of tuberculosis.

1892-1893
- Ronald remains as headmaster at Ravenscroft. Little or no correspondence from this time.

1894
- September - Ronald gives up his position at Ravenscroft and moves back to England.

1897
- Ronald marries Constance Mary Margaret Robertson in England.

1933
- Ronald MacDonald dies on July 13, 1933 at Earles Court, London.

Bibliography

The American, English and Venezuelan Trading and Commercial. Company *The Emigrant's Vade-mecum or Guide to the "Price Grant" in Venezuelan Guayana*. London: Messrs. Trubner and company, Pasternoster Row, E.C., 1868

Bailey, David Coleman. *Fashionable Asheville: Volumes 1 & 2*. Charleston, SC: Book Surge, 2004.

Bowie, Walter Russell. *The Master of the Hill: A Biography of John Meets*. New York: Dodd, Mead and Company, 1917.

Chase, Nan K. *Asheville: A History*. Jefferson, NC: McFarland & Company, Publishers, 2007.

Chapin, George H. *Health Resorts of the South: containing numerous engravings descriptive of the most desirable health and pleasure resorts of the Southern states*. Boston: George H. Chapin, 1889.

Dykeman, Wilma. *The French Broad*. Newport, TN: Wake stone Books, 1955.

Ehle, John. *The Road*. Knoxville, TN: University of Tennessee, 1998.

Greenberg, Sue and Kahn, Jan. *Asheville Volume Two (NC)*. Mount Pleasant, SC: Arcadia Publishing, 1997.

Hanna, Alfred Jackson and Hanna, Kathryn Abbey. *Confederate Exiles in Venezuela*. Tuscaloosa, Alabama: Confederate Publishing Company, Inc 1960

Harshaw, Lou. *Asheville: Mountain Majesty*. Asheville, NC: Bright Mountain Books, 2007.

Hein, Rolland. *George MacDonald: Victorian Mythmaker*. Nashville, TN: Star Song Publishing Group, 1993.

Hewison, Robert. *Ruskin and Oxford: The Art of Education*. Oxford: Clarendon Press, 1996.

Hewison, Robert; Warrell, Ian; and Wildman, Steven. Ruskin, *Turner and The Pre-Raphaelites*. London: Tate Gallery, 2000.

Horne, Gerald. *The Deepest South: The United States, Brazil, and the African Slave Trade*. New York: New York University Press, 2007.

Langley, Joan and Langley, Wright. *Yesterday's Asheville*. Miami: E. A. Seemann Publishing, 1975.

Manthorne, Katherine E. and Coffey, John. *The Landscapes of Louis Rémy Mignot: A Southern Painter Abroad*. Raliegh, NC: North Carolina Museum of Art, 1996

McDaniel, Douglas Stuart. *Asheville (NC) (Images of America)*. Mount Pleasant, SC: Arcadia Publishing, 2004.

Newall, Christopher. *The Grosvenor Gallery Exhibitions: Change and continuity in the Victorian art world*. Cambridge: Cambridge University Press, 1995.

Raeper, William. *George MacDonald*. Batavia, IL: Lion Publishing, 1987.

Sadler, Glenn Edward. *An Expression of Character: The Letters of George MacDonald* Grand Rapids, MI: W. B. Eerdmans Pub. Co., 1994.

Tessier, Mitzi Schaden. *Asheville: A Pictorial History*. Marceline, MO: Donning Company, 1982.

George MacDonald Websites and Journals

The Golden Key - *http://www.george-macdonald.com/*

George MacDonald Informational Web - *http://georgemacdonald.info/*

Northwind: A Journal of George MacDonald Studies

John Pennington, Editor, Department of English, St. Norbert College
100 Grant Street, De Pere, WI 54115-2099 USA
Email: john.pennington@snc.edu.
http://www.snc.edu/english/northwind.html

Wingfold : A Literary Quarterly

Barbara Amell, Editor, 3925 SE 39th #1, Portland, OR 97202
Email: b_amell@prodigy.net
http://pages.prodigy.net/b_amell/wingfold1.html

Appendix A

The following letter from Alfred Blandy to Jefferson Davis is in Box 4 of the Jefferson Davis Family Collection at the Museum of the Confederacy in Richmond, VA. Dated "Jan. 2" we know, from other historical records of the Davis family that the letter was written in 1869. The Davis family had moved to England from Canada for Jefferson Davis to find employment or other means of support for his family. After spending time in Warwickshire, the Davis family moved to London, first staying with the Blandy family at 57 Gloucester Place, before leasing their own apartment at 18 Upper Gloucester, Dorset. From the letter we deduce that Jefferson and Varina were away from London (other records show that they were in France at this time), and had left their children in the care of the Blandys. Below is the letter in its entirety:

57 Gloucester Place,
Hyde Park, W.
Jan. 2nd.

Dear Mr. Davis,

I have had two interviews with Mr. Feason about your property in Canada which I am afraid leads to very little practical good— He says that it appears to him to be a better plan to find purchasers in C as there is now plenty of Capital—More he says it would be difficult to find any monied man who would buy what he knew nothing about. He stated he had agents in all part of C & a very good man near your property & that he would interest them in disposing of it, in advancing this end, but he decidedly thinks the purchase would best be made there, as most likely to bring a just-price. He wished to know if you had put any valuation upon it, to which I could give no answer—In concluding I must say he showed the greatest possible desire to facilitate this thing & has already written to C—and he may be able to do something in this way.

Your little family are all well & happy, of course except slight colds which Maggy[a] & Jeff[b] have. The little girl is full of her little fairy tales with her expressive manners every afternoon. At present she is out walking with the nurses. Miss Howell[c] has gone to St. Paul's with Jeff and Mrs. B. Willy[d] is in the park with nurses & Maggy[a] is playing as hard as possible with Lulu[e] so you can fell assured of the happy state of them all, at least as much so as a sweet family can be in the absence of their very good & kind parents. Our household is very sad in your absence & immense wonderments as to what you are doing & how you are enjoying yourself is almost their sole occupation. Hoping that everything you meet & see will bring a new joy to your hearts & that these changes may renew a tender & true hope & with kind remembrances to Mrs. Davis, believe me honored sir, your most humble friend & obedient servant,

Alfred A. Blandy

[a] Margaret Howell Davis Hayes (1855-1905) – eldest daughter of Jefferson & Varina Banks Howell Davis.

[b] Jefferson Davis, Jr. (1857-1878) – second born son and namesake of Jefferson & Varina Banks Howell Davis.

[c] Margaret Graham Howell (1846-1909) – sister of Varina Howell Davis.

[d] William Howell Davis (1861-1874) – son of Jefferson & Varina Banks Howell Davis.

[e] Louise Virenda Blandy MacDonald (1857-1890) – daughter of Alfred A. & Ozillah Louisa Harris Blandy – and future wife of Ronald MacDonald.

NOTE: The Blandy's had a baby daughter born in 1869. They appropriately named their daughter: "Varina Anne Jefferson Davis Blandy". "Winnie" as she was affectionately called is mentioned often in this story of Ronald and Louise MacDonald.

Appendix B
Ronald MacDonald's Plays

"All the Difference"
Opened January 9, 1896 – St. George's Hall, London.

Written by Ronald, this play was presented in conjunction with another play, *"A Complete Change"*, a farce written by his brother Bernard. Ronald and Bernard produced and acted in both of their productions.

The plot: *"John Oakdene falls in love with Kitty Marchmont, but the lady entertains a firm belief that poverty and happiness do not go together, and as her suitor is a poor man she refuses to marry him. She repents of her action, however, when she learns that the property of a deceased uncle has been bequeathed to her, and she gives her lover to understand that her answer to his suit would, under these altered circumstances, be a different one. Oakdene is, however, too proud to become the poor husband of a wealthy wife; and it is not until the discovery is made that Kitty's defunct relative has executed a later will in favor of his nephew, Geoffrey Chalgrave, that the lovers are rendered happy."*[123]

Cast:

Geoffrey Chalgrave	- Ronald MacDonald
John Oakdene	- Henry Arncliffe
Mr. Vanbrugh	- Arthur Rowlands
Squales, a valet	- Bernard MacDonald
Mrs. Stephen Oakdene	- Annie Stallman
Kitty Marchmont	- Maud Abbott

---

123 From newspaper article: "New Plays at St. George's Hall", *The Era*, London: Saturday, January 18, 1896.

"The Eleventh Hour"
Opened September 14, 1896 – Prince of Wales Theatre, London

Written in collaboration with H. A. Saintsbury, this play was a sensational hit and toured England for two years. Noted for it's elaborate and numerous (seven) scenery sets, this play was especially notable because of it's "Great Sensation Scene, illustrating a dynamite explosion!"[124]

The plot: The central character is Mark Warnock who, in an effort for revenge against Robert Fordyce, a local subversive who had killed Warnock's brother, infiltrates innumerable subversive secret societies. For many years Warnock pursued his enemy, but to soothe his conscience from the sin of taking part in the work of secret organizations, he keeps police fully informed of their proceedings. When the curtain rises, however, his thirst for vengeance is not as fierce as of yore, and he has assumed the responsibilities and quiet life of postmaster at Richmond. His pretty daughter Vesta has brought her influence to bear, and as far as he (Mark Warnock) is concerned, the feud is at an end. But fate is stronger than the man. Vesta is loved by Francis Millthorpe, the nephew of Lord Edgbaston, the Home Secretary, who seeks her hand in marriage. Mark has scruples however, and will not permit the young aristocrat to marry Vesta unwitting her father's past history, so he unbosoms himself of the past and its story. But Millthorpe, who is a gentleman in more than mere name, persuades Warnock once more to act the part of the spy, and to keep the Government informed of the developments of a great Fenian plot of which word has reached them. In the end, Warnock assists in saving the life of the Home Secretary by aiding him to escape his house safety just minutes before the subsequent explosion.[125]

---

124 From newspaper advertisement: *The Era*, London: Saturday, March 20, 1897.
125 Summarized from newspaper article: The Era, London: Saturday, September 19, 1896.

Cast:

Lord Edgbaston	- Ronald MacDonald
Francis Millthorpe	- A. Steffens-Hardy
Hon. Edger Fitzherbert	- Chisholm Taylor
Il Conte Di Vascari	- Alec Forbes
Robert Fordyce	- Leonard Outran
Jules Gautran	- Wallace Douglas
Sergio Stoilowski	- Wilfred H. Franks
Patrick O'Kelly	- Stanislaus Calhaem
Antonio Semeria	- C. J. Watson
Hans Deidricht	- Henry B. Lewis
Sam Tucknott	- Chas. E. Warne
Inspector Breckbridge	- George Newton
Inspector Colwick	- Frank Nichols
Johnstone	- R. D. Egerton
Wilkins	- Charles Mallory
Winterton	- W. M. Sellick
Brownlow	- George Newbound
Mark Warnock	- H. A. Saintsbury
Vesta Warnock	- Constance Robertson
The Duchess of Sloborough	- Nora Carroll
Lady Jane Hartington	- Isobel Wilson
Lady Violet Hartington	- Margaret Wilson
The Countess of Malcontowers	- Kitty Stranack
The Hon. Miss Cholmondeley	-Florence Lattimore
Nora Sullivan	- Marianne Caldwell

"The Sword of the King"
Opened October 6, 1902 – Wallack's Theatre, Broadway, NY.
Closed November 1902.[126]

The plot: The Sword of the King is a story of the time when William of Orange was making his sturdy fight for the English crown. The heroine tells the tale. She is Philippa Drayton, a brave and lovely girl, whose father sides with the Prince of Orange. The character of Philippa Drayton is engaging, and the story is full of exciting action and adventure.[127]

Produced by Maurice Campbell – Written by Ronald MacDonald

Directed by Eugene W Presby and Henrietta Crosman

Scenic Design by P. J. McDonald and L. C. Young

Cast:

Gertrude Bennett; Henry Bergman; Frederick C. Bertrand; Sheridan Block; Aubrey Boucicault; Henrietta Crosman; Edwin Fowler; Henry Gunson; William Herbert; Barton Hill; F. J. McCarty; Addison Pitt; Arthur Shaw; and Ida Vernon.

"Jocelyn the Jester" in one act.
Opened March 4, 1907 at the Crystal Palace, London and played at the Grand, Croyton, 1910.

Cast:

Jocelyn Savage	H. A. Saintsbury
Sir Giles Wedderburn	C. H. Croker-King
Percival Kingston, Esq.	C. W. Standing
Chirrup	Leonard Calvert
Martha Wimpling	Violet Vivian
Lucinda	Dorthea Desmond

---

126 See Internet Broadway database, www.imdb.com.

127 *The American Monthly Review of Reviews* v.22 Jul-Dec 1900. edited by Albert Shaw. Published by *Review of Reviews*., 1900. page 760. See also: *New York Times* article: "Miss Crosman's Melodrama at Wallack's", October 2, 1902.

"The Frame" sketch in one act.
Opened March 20, 1911 at the Court Theatre, London.

Cast:

Anatolio Montolieri	H. A. Saintsbury
Celestine Lebas	Lucy Wilson
Mme. Fanchat	Clare Greet

"The Chief of Staff" sketch in one act.
Opened at the Lyric Theatre, London.
Closed February 13, 1910.

Cast:

Gen. de Solatierra	W. Haviland
Col. Stephen Cavendish	Lewis Waller
Major Dennis O'Driscoll	A. E. George
Guillermo Herrero	Shiel Barry
Sergeant Baltazar	Cronin Wilson
Pedro Costanza	S. J. Warmington
Jaime	Reginald Dane
Marcos	Caton Woodville
Fraequito	George Courtney
A Despatch rider	Patrick Digan
Engracia de Solatierra	Auriol Lec
Iduna de Solatierra	Evelyn D'Alroy
Lola	Madge Titheradge

"The Red Herring" play in four acts.
Opened May 1, 1911 at the Court Theatre, London.

Plot: Casimir de Mont-Lussac, adept at international intrigue, stages a minor international incident as a "red herring" to avert an even worse potential international incident. Mont-Lussac's righteous deception has ramifications for the foreign affairs of his country, but also for the affairs of his heart.[128]

Cast:

Casimir de Mont-Lussac	Leon Quartermaine
Mr. Rendle	Benedick Butler
Clara	Beatrice Chester
James Adderley Canfield	J. Wilcox
Marquis of Cottersdale	H. L. Leyton
Marchioness of Cottersdale	Mary Forbes
Major Thwaites	Cecil Kinnaird
Charles Sufflick	Arnold Lucy
Myraphne Ffolliot-Wilson	Esmé Hubbard
Hon. Evelyn St. Elvyn	Georgette de Serville
Casimir de Mont-Lussac	Leon Quartermaine
Footman	Ralph Gaffagan
Mayfield	Margaret Damer
Thomas	Walter Cross
Alex. McIlwrath	Alec F. Thompson
Inspector of Police	H. B. Tabberer

---

128 Synopsis by Dale Wayne Slusser.

Appendix C
Books by Ronald MacDonald

RONALD MACDONALD - FROM THE BOOKMAN

The Sword of The King

> 1900- UK- John Murray: London
> 1900- US- The Century Company: New York

"The Sword of the King," by Ronald Macdonald, is another tale of adventure according to the present fashion, and a much better fashion, too, than that of a few years ago. It is the maiden effort of the author and promises well, for the interest is maintained until the end of the book, the sentiment being genuine and wholesome, the characters naturally drawn, and the plot skillful. Mr. Macdonald has imitated the literary style of the latter part of the seventeenth century, and with considerable success, though it is a trifle overdone. For instance, a phrase like "love *to* his book" seems clumsy even for that age, and Milton and the Bible certainly say "love of," while "hold *in* this belief" is unnecessary, when the Bible two generations before said "hold to the one and despise the other." The tale is told by the heroine in the first person, and the fiction that it is a woman's story is so well maintained that one forgets that the author belongs to the other sex. [129]

---

129 "Public Opinion –Comprehensive Summary of the Press Thoroughout the World on All Important Current Topics, Volume XXIX." July, 1900—December, 1900. Public Opinion: Astor, New York, 1900. page 153.

God Save The King

1901- UK- Hutchinson & Co.: London, Paternoster Row.
1901- US- The Century Company: New York
2007- US- Kessinger Publishing: Whitefish, Montana

"A story in autobiographical form and antique style concerning Charles II, who is aided in his escape after the battle of Worcester by the boy hero and girl heroine. Romance and adventure, with keen delineation of character, abound, the tale culminating in a remarkable scene in which the king, armed with evil intent on one of his mad escapades, is yet saved to honor by the very man and woman, who, as children, had befriended him. The novel has unusual brilliancy and an impressionistic color and picturesqueness which render it truly artistic."[130]

Camilla Faversham

1903- UK- Hutchinson & Co.: London, Paternoster Row.

A domestic novel in which the story is good and well told and the character-drawing a special feature. Camilla, the principal character, is the daughter of a gentleman who has lost caste. She works on her own account and despises men : she meets Haldane and becomes engaged, but they quarrel, and Camilla continues her work. Trouble follows, but there is a satisfactory ending.[131]

The Sea Maid

1906- UK- Methuen Publishing: London
1906- US- Henry Holt & Company: New York
2007- US- Kessinger Publishing: Whitefish, Montana

"...Dean of Beckminster and his ailing wife sailed for the antipodes in 1883, and for nearly a quarter of a century remained

---

130 "The Literary World: A Monthly Review of Current Literature", Volume XXXIII, January-December 1902. H. Hames & Company: Boston, April 1, 1902. page 60.

131 Publisher's Advertisement in: *The Yellow Van*, by Richard Whiteing. Hutchinson & Co.: Paternoster Row, London, 1903.

unheard from, and naturally mourned as dead. As a matter of fact, they had been shipwrecked upon an uncharted island, and so contrived to adapt themselves to circumstances that when they are discovered they are found to be leading a reasonably comfortable existence. We hasten to mention that there is a daughter, born upon the island, and now grown to beautiful womanhood without ever having seen other human beings than her parents. This Miranda is the '' sea maid '' of the title, and when her Ferdinand turns up, the natural consequences follow. His appearance is contrived by a mutiny on board a steamer in the Australian trade, with the marooning of officers and passengers upon the same unknown island, which happens to be conveniently at hand. Here is a piquant situation, and it is developed with ingenious success, albeit with a certain extravagance of humor.. For sheer entertainment this story is one of the best of the year, and it is by no means devoid of the qualities that appeal to the literary sense."[132]

A Human Trinity

1907- UK- Methuen Publishing: London
2007- US- Kessinger Publishing: Whitefish, Montana

"The whole of A Human Trinity is divided, like the dog's-eared Gaul of our schoolboy-days, into three parts. Part I., "The Three," introduces a mother, father and son, the two last of whom are unaware of each other's existence. Part II., " The Two," harks back to the beginning of things, and shows how it came about that Tony Le Dane was born the son of Randolph Bethune, the traveler, and Lady Mary Frozier, the artist (whom he supposed to be his aunt); and Part III., "The Trinity," or Three in One, explains how Tony, by insisting on the marriage of his newly found parents, fashioned of their three lives an isosceles triangle…."[133]

---

132 "The Dial", volume XL January 1-June 16, 1906. The Dial Company: Chicago, IL, page 265.

133 From a review in: "The Punch", volume CXXXII. Punch: London, April 24,1907. page 288.

The Election of Isabel

1907- UK- Edward Arnold Publishers: London

It was inevitable that the claims of the ' Suffragettes ' should afford material for a novel, but few authors could have attacked the subject in a lighter or happier vein than Mr. Macdonald. Lady Isabel Fenchurch, the daughter of the Duke of Hounsditch, is depicted as a perfectly charming woman with an infatuation for the ' Feminist Movement.' She marries Charles Lawless on the understanding that it is merely a matter of convenience, that he will supply her with funds for ' the cause,' and give her absolute freedom. He hopes in time to win her love, and accepts half a loaf as better than no bread. Then follows a host of difficulties arising from the situation, all treated most humorously, and culminating in an election, in which Lady Isabel and her husband are rival candidates. It would not be fair to reveal the finale ; the book should be read mainly for its amusing qualities, but here and there are glimpses of a more serious appreciation of this burning question.[134]

The Carcase

1909- UK- Everett & Company: London

"In this finely conceived story, Mr. Ronald MacDonald deals with the case of a young man with a weak heart and a hereditary tendency to alcoholism, who was heir to great possessions, provided that he attained the age of twenty-five. Although his relatives were either rich or in comfortable circumstances, yet in spite of this, nearly all of them, from his mother downwards, were from sordid motives bent on his moral and physical undoing. How far they succeeded, and how far they were baffled in their nefarious designs through the heroic devotion of his wife, is told with amazing psychological insight."[135]

---

134 Publisher's advertisement: *Memoirs of Mistral* by Constance Elizabeth Maud. Edward Arnold: London, 1907.

135 From Everett & Co.Publisher's advertisement: "British Books in Print". J. Whitaker & Sons: London, 1910. page 21.

The Red Herring

1910- UK- Everett & Company: London

Casimir de Mont-Lussac, adept at international intrigue, stages a minor international incident as a "red herring" to avert an even worse potential international incident. Mont-Lussac's righteous deception has ramifications for the foreign affairs of his country, but also for the affairs of his heart.[136]

The First of the Ebb

1911- UK- Everett & Company: London
1911- UK- George Newnes Ltd. Edition: London[137]
1911- UK- G. Bell and Sons: London. This edition issued for circulation in India and the Colonies only.[138]

"A well told and stirring romance of the French Revolution.—*The Times*"[139]

Raymond Lanchester

1912- UK- John Murray: London
1913- UK- John Murray: London

Raymond Lanchester is a modern knight of chivalry, who, in loyalty to an unfaithful wife and for love of his little son, takes upon his own shoulders the burden of another's crime. The clever amateur detective work of his young actress friend, "Divvy - Di," brings to light a writer of anonymous letters who is spreading misery far and wide. The story ends with the reconciliation of friends long parted and the well-earned happiness of Lanchester and "Diwy-Di."[140]

---

136 Synopsis by Dale Wayne Slusser, November 11, 2008.

137 From bookseller on: http://www.biblioz.com/search.php.

138 Ibid.

139 Publisher's advertisement in: *The Red Grange* by Molesworth. Everett & Co.: London, 1913. page 256.

140 *The Publisher's Weekly*, Feb. 1, 1913. Volume LXXXIII. Offices of the Publisher's Weekly: New York, 1913.

Gambier's Advocate

1914- UK- Everett & Company: London
1914-US- John Lane Co.: New York
2007- US- Kessinger Publishing: Whitefish, Montana

"Stephen Gambier, barrister, the hero of Mr. MacDonald's new and interesting novel, certainly found himself in an unusual and decidedly awkward position. Yet his lot in life was apparently all that could be desired: one of the rising men in his profession, with excellent chances of obtaining a seat in Parliament and engaged to a wealthy and charming girl—who could help envying him? Which only goes to prove the old saying about the deceitfulness of appearances. And no sooner did it begin to seem probable that he would emerge triumphant from an embarrassing situation than he became involved in new and far more serious trouble—trouble with which the world speedily became acquainted, and forthwith a large part of it turned its back on him. However, he behaved like a gentleman through all his difficulties, and very nearly deserved the reward he finally received. ...."Gambier's Advocate' is a clever story"[141]

The Green Handkerchief

1922- UK- Cecil Palmer: London

Christabel's true love has left England to sail to the wilds of South America, perhaps never to be seen again. Another suitor persuades her to marry him instead. Christabel marrys Mr. Bazalgette for money, not to gain it but to give it! Christabel gives Mr. Bazalgette, her new lawyer husband, her recently inherited sixty thousand pounds, to keep the firm afloat after his mismanagement of funds and speculative ventures almost ruined him and his partner, Mr. Yardlip. Christabel proves to be a loving wife and true heroine, as not long after marrying, her husband dies leaving her to support her two stepchildren, Stanislas and Dolores. How will she support her step children in the manner to which they are accustomed, without revealing the dire financial straits in which their father has left them? Having sunk her own money into the so

---

141 Excerpt from newspaper article: *The New York Times*, New York. September 20, 1914.

far unprofitable, speculative housing schemes of her late husband, she devises a scheme to make money. Since childhood, Christabel has been imagining and "telling" stories, but alas she has not the gift of "writing." So she enlists the help of Oxford don, Aristobulos Demanga as her "secretary" to secretly turn her stories into publishable material. Needing to write what sells, Christabel assumes various pennames and produces, what the unsuspecting local vicar calls "lurid twaddle". All turns out for good and is revealed at the end, including the fact that Christabel has the true gift of making fairytales. All are surprised that the author of that "lurid twaddle" is also the author of the sweet, insightful and popular novel, *The Laughing Elf*.

The Laughing Elf

> 1922- UK- Blackwell: London
> 1932- UK- Cecil Palmer: London

A fairy tale/fable about the necessity of both sorrow and joy in our lives. This story also plays a role in Ronald's novel, *The Green Handkerchief*, also published in 1922. See an excerpt from this story in Appendix D.

Ambrotox and Limping Dick

> 1920-UK- with Philip MacDonald as: Oliver Fleming

A mystery/thriller co-written with his son to help him launch his future career as an author. This book is now available as a free E-Book at: http://www.gutenburg.org/etext/20119

The Spandau Quid

> 1923- UK- with Philip MacDonald as: Oliver Fleming

Another mystery/thriller co-written with his son to help Philip with his chosen career of becoming an author.

MacDonald, Ronald. "George MacDonald: A Personal Note." In *From A Northern Window: Papers Critical Historical and Imaginative*, edited by Fredrick Watson and Ian Maclaren, pp. 55-113. James Nisbet, 1911.

PHILIP MACDONALD, (RONALD'S SON)
AUTHOR AND SCREENWRITER

Philip Macdonald (1899-1981) also wrote as Oliver Fleming, Anthony Lawless and Martin Porlock. He served with the cavalry regiment in Mesopotamia during World War 1 and later trained horses for the army.

He wrote some very important and influential books, and his third book *The Link* (1930) was ingeniously plotted and remains even today a key book, not least for being one of the first books published in the Collins Crime Club. *Murder Gone Mad* (1931) also merits particular attention as a Golden Age classic and was selected by John Dickson Carr as one of the 'Ten Greatest Detective Novels'. In 1953 and 1956, Macdonald was recognised by the Mystery Writers of America, who awarded him the Edgar Allan Poe award for his short stories.

information from - http://www.fantasticfiction.co.uk/m/philip-macdonald/

Appendix D

THE LAUGHING ELF

by Ronald MacDonald

THE LAUGHING

ONCE upon a time, when men knew less and fairies little more than now, there was an Elf that was unhappy. No fairy loved him, none played with him twice, and few even made as if they saw him passing by.

Fairyland being the only country that he knew, though little of it, he could not have told you where he was, nor who he was, nor why he was. And the *who* was the doubt which most troubled him. If he could but know that, he thought, he might perhaps discover his *what-for-ness.*

Had you and I then seen his little crumpled face with its funny, sharp ears, we should not have laughed; and when in a pool or some clear rivulet, he would examine it himself, he could not smile; for the frown he saw reflected was of puckered perplexity, showing neither judgment nor disgust.

And from this contemplation he would turn always to renew his elfish quest of he knew not what.

Sometimes, however, awaking from dreams.. he could not remember, this anxious Elf would be filled for a while with belief that discovery had been very near; so it came about that a little thing in him, which he did not yet know for hope, tempted him often and yet more often to break his wandering search by curling himself down to sleep in any place which he fitted softly enough.

One morning, in early dawn, he awoke to find he had lain down at the edge of a dark wood of pine-trees that stood upon the very border of fairyland. He opened his crinkled eyelids to peer out over the rim of the small, turf-padded hollow that had made his bed.

Towards him, from the gentle bands of grey light, brooding over the birth-place of the sun, came Sorrow. The cloud of her black garment first swinging out soft and thin, and then, with her slackening approach, closing back about her, dark and heavy to the feet.

Her name the Elf did not know; but when he was so near that he could see her eyes, his little heart fell and sank away from him until it seemed to melt into the earth.

Never seeing his small face staring at her from below, Sorrow gazed far above him toward the dark wall of the pine-wood, until the elf turned about to know, even though he feared, what it was that she saw or waited to see.

Out of the wood, dim at first, but soon sure and splendid, came Joy. At sight of the dark form which he did not know, Joy's pace was quickened until Sorrow and he looked each into the other's eyes.

Softly and secretly the Elf sat down upon the brink of his hollow, with his back toward the growing light, and looked up into the strange faces of this pair that met in the dawn. For his heart had come back to him out of the ground, so that never again should he be afraid.

Although he did not know who they were, he yet said to himself, looking from the one countenance to the other: "It is a marvel: neither knows the other, but neither could know himself if the other were not! Are they enemies, or do they belong together?"

Deeper and deeper above him gazed the two pairs of eyes. The two heads were bent together, as if across some barrier between their bodies; and the Elf, looking downward from those two faces saw for the first time, standing breast-high between Sorrow and Joy, a little white fellow whose golden head was shining, even before a ray from the sun could gild it.

When they kissed above him, this naked stranger touched them with a hand apiece, and they looked down upon him, stepping apart.

"Who art thou?" asked Sorrow, bending over, so that some little wind swept a fold of her robe about him. And the elf saw how those slender white limbs shone through the blackness.

Then, before Sorrow had her answer:

"Who art thou, shining there? – asked Joy. With his right hand the little fellow touched Sorrow upon the arm.

"I am your his-ness," he said, fixing his eyes upon Joy.

"For you," he said, as his left hand touched Joy's arm, "I am your her-ness."

Then those two looked the more each at the other, asking, as with one voice, of him they no longer regarded:

"But thou—thou thyself—who art thou?" Then the Elf saw that the loose billow of Sorrow's robe fell back, so that the whiteness of him whose name they sought shone, with the nearing sun, brighter even than before.

"I am not myself a *me,*" he answered. " But when I am grown up, I am going to be the me-ness and the you-ness of all the world."

The light grew, sending now upward spears to the soft grey clouds. So the Elf saw the tears which ran down the three faces of his worship, and above them such a shining of the eyes which shed them as made him cast down his own from the brightness. And as he looked down he saw a tiny, yellow-cupped flower at his knee, at that moment opening its night-tightened lips.

"Those tears," he thought, "are wasted, if they do not mingle," and, plucking the flower for a cup, he made shift to catch with it one shining drop from each passion.

Then it was that the sun shot along the earth his first level ray, piercing grass-blades and tight heather-bells with all their wet jewelry of quivering diamonds. And the Elf turned his back upon the three that wept, and lifted his slender-stemmed, yellow-bowled goblet into the sunbeam.

Through cup and liquor shone the light, and he saw a colour which you and I believe in, although we have not seen it ever in prism nor in dewdrop—saw it, and never saw again, but always.

So he lifted his cup and drank what it held, knowing a savour which has not faded even to this day.

He drank and fell asleep in his grass-lined pocket of the hillside. Sleeping, he dreamed of the heart of things, and, when he awoke, remembered how one was nothing, and another was nothing, and how a third could not alone exist; and how yet the three were all and everybody.

So well did he see into this clear mystery, knowing all its ins and outs better than the most industrious of school-girls her tables of multiplication, that he leapt to his feet and began running down the hill in the moonlight, saying in his quick-beating heart:

"I will go and tell them—tell them—tell everybody!"

He ran until he came to a wide green place, in a village of men and houses asleep.

In the middle of the green he stood panting, and scratching his hot, pointed ears in perplexity.

He must tell them of the three nothings that were everything: of the new colour; and of the white limbs of that little fellow, which shone through the smoky black garment that was not his.

But how tell?

How to tell the best tale that ever there was, to ears shut in sleep— and a tale for which, after all, the words were not yet fashioned?

A strange passion panted in his breast and throbbed in his throat.

"A tale which will not be told; a tale with no words; a tale for ears that cannot listen and for heads that do not wish to know! A tale which must get out—a tale that will not stay at home!"

So ran his thought, while a sort of tickling came to the throbbing in his throat. This was absurd; and, since he knew no such word, yet felt its very inmost meaning, he fell sitting to the grass, flung back his head, and sent out over the world the first laughing it ever knew: for he had found, without knowing he had found it, the language for telling at least the beginning of the story which he had seen.

Before his last slumber he had seen the secret of the likenesses, the unlikenesses, and all the degrees of all the differences which are among all men and things. One sip from the yellow cup made him intoxicated with the love of the great picture, and when he awoke, that new colour which is not found even in the rainbow was his forever.

So he lifted his voice to tell all the world, and many folk of that village heard the new language of laughter.

JOY AND THE BUILDER

In that same village dwelt a man who was a builder—the same who one day would build the fair house which arose behind the Gates of Welcome.

And because he thought much upon his work, and, indeed, would often dream the night through among visions of palaces, homesteads, castles and cottages, surpassing all that his bodily eye had seen for beauty conjoined with *fitness,* his spirit was sometimes sad with knowing that, of the few men in those parts who had need of a new house, there was none that truly understood convenience nor loved beauty.

He had even dreamed, in the days before the Elf came, of one who came to him, saying: "Build me a house." And this dream, though he would dream it often, never went further; for with the joy of the command came the end of sleep, leaving him with the pale daylight shining upon the two temples of the village, and a day's work of directing his craftsmen who were mending a barn, or digging foundations for some ugly dwelling.

Now, of those two temples which he saw every day from his window, the one was built heavily of great stone blocks, very square and hopeless to look upon, having a door midway of each side, and square windows above. And within was an altar at each corner of the square floor, so that no worshipper looked in the face of another.

But the second was a great gilded temple, like a globe sunk halfway into the earth. There were many windows, like sleepy eyes, and but two doors in all its single wall; the one for entrance, narrow to the bare width of a man's shoulders, and the other for going out, whence four might come abreast. Here, in the floor's middle, was an altar, the very centre of ring upon ring of curved benches, to seat a circled multitude so each man might see the face of every other.

And the builder knew the creed of each temple as well as he could have sketched on his tablet the shape of the building which housed it.

For in the earliest days which he could recall, his mother would take him on the middle day of the week to the round, yellow-shining temple where the congregation adored an effigy of its own qualities, calling this image MAN, and where the faithful spoke of themselves as

WE, and of their gathering place as The House of Us.

From his tenth year, his father would take him, upon the last day of each week, to the square temple where, in short invocations divided by long silences, men worshipped a force which could help neither them nor itself a power of which, indeed, they knew so little that it was named among them IT—IT Inevitable and Supreme.

And recalling each parent's solemn observance of religion, he would wonder now in manhood that they had never found in their difference of belief cause of dispute nor any unhappiness. But he would remember further how he had asked his father who was it did send the rain upon the earth.

"Do we not," his father answered, "always say IT raineth, IT bloweth, IT sendeth the heat and the cold ?"

"And what," asked the child, "is IT'?"

"Who knows?" said the man.

But the boy persisted.

"IT! Is IT good? Is IT bad? Is IT like unto us, my father?

"'Tis taught in the temple, my son, that in no wise is IT like unto us; and therefore is our measuring of good and evil altogether strange unto IT."

"Shall I know more of it, when I am grown to a man?" asked the son.

"Because we cannot see IT, my son, we call IT blind; nor hear IT, therefore deaf. IT is and IT must be, but without knowledge we worship."

Silenced, yet in no wise answered, the boy, coming three days thereafter from the gilded dome with his mother, plied her in turn with childish inquiries. And when she told him in terms lame rather than simple her temple's easy doctrine of a single, widespread spirit of MAN, immanent in all things and all men, he asked again – Is that Spirit good?"

"There are good men, and good women and good children, like you, my son," she replied. "Therefore must the Spirit of MAN be a good spirit."

"There are bad men also, mother," began the boy; but when he saw a frowning of pain on her forehead, he kept the conclusion of his reasoning within his own mind.

His father's IT was a thing little adorable, since was found therein no knowledge and no goodness; and that the spirit to which his mother bowed was mixed of good and evil, so that a child might not, for any light her temple could let shine, discover a difference between the bad thing and the good.

Man-grown and orphaned, he brooded on the shapeless desire he had between his father's seeking closeness to other men in the bond of their common fate, and his mother's comfort in the common suffering of a community of resistance or palliation.

Each parent had taken some little pleasure from life; much, he knew, they had given to their son; for they, being gone, yet showed him by their absence what men and women may be to one another. And yet this measuring of his loss taught him further that the thing unnamed, after which, boy and man, he longed, was above and beyond all that they had to give.

For even in those days there was found, here and there among men, one that held in his dim soul knowledge of a need, a lacking; a thirst, as it were, after a liquid of which the golden radiance and immortal impulse were only perceived as the sun's light through the sealed eyelids of some new-born puppy.

Just so the builder knew not what he sought, but knew very surely that always was he seeking. For the Elf had not yet looked upon the meeting of Joy with Sorrow on the hillside, between moorland and forest.

Yet there grew stronger in him the belief that this thirst he had was the need of the temple which was square, and also that which was round; and that, unless he should find what he fumbled for, seeking without direction, he would never see, even in his dream, the beauty of the house he had been commanded to build.

Three times in the years since he was alone had he said, to himself – "At last I have found it." And each time that which he had found died in his fingers; and of each dead thing he said as he laid it aside – "This was a good thing, but still do I seek."

Then there came a day when the man's spirit lay exceeding heavy in his breast; and it was the same day upon which, in the last hour, the Elf laughed.

And the builder stirred himself, and said: "I will draw shapes and plans of houses until I be weary. And perhaps I will find among them a form that tells me what I know not."

He drew and planned, measuring and shaping such castles and temples, houses end workshops as he wished that men would command of him. When the night came he worked by candle light. So that in the end he was weary indeed, and a voice cried within his darkened heart: "In what are these better than those which they have?"

Weary and low of spirit, the builder fell asleep as the moon was rising, with his arms for a pillow between his head and the table.

Through the walls of his slumber there came to him music, which was the laughing of the Elf upon the village green. And once more his dream was upon him, of the command that was given: "Build for me a house!"

And the music, which was laughter leaking through to the chamber of his dream, did so interpret and make plain to him that command that he knew in that very stroke of time what manner of house he must build.

Then he opened his eyes, and looked from his window, and saw two temples clear in the moonlight. Not knowing or heeding the newness of his own utterance, he laughed at the gilded roundness, and said,

"One is thrust up through the earth, and sticks half-way. But the other temple, with its low, thick walls like patient shoulders of stone is pushed down into earth, yet is too strong for burial complete."

Then having tasted his own laughter once more,

"But Joy's Temple," he cried (having perceived in the very finding of his treasure the name that was written there) "— Joy's Temple shall soar like a flame drawn upward and leaping for ever."

Then, in the growing light of the new day, he began working with his pencils and rulers and compasses to plan that house he had so often been commanded to conceive and build. And now, while the scheme of beauty took form upon his parchment, he was so little weary that he wondered if he was awake or in the second chapter of his old dream. But, awaking from slumber, fearing that all his joy and labour were lost, the builder laughed aloud with great comfort to find his work lying about him in sheet upon sheet of finished design. And when he examined them, he knew that no dream was so good as this work of his.

For he conceived the Temple of Joy arising from mighty foundations in walls and columns of stone, stronger than fate and lovelier than any temple of man. Seen from afar, it reached upward with great arms ascending to slender fingers of aspiration, clear-stamped upon their background of light – whether grey cloud, azure of summer noon, or deep, star-jewelled blue of midnight. Drawing nearer, you would see a fair pattern in stone, light as foliage and strong as steel. The strength of arched window and door, the loving weight and deft angle of buttress and keystone; and, as the eye went upward, each window lighter and more up-reaching than the last.

But, upon coming so near that his eyes might embrace in a glance just two windows, a man might begin to read the story written in the stones of these walls; yet not until he had spent the leisure of half a lifetime in that loving glance should he come to the end of that book.

For by the builder's chisel should be wrought in this great upheaval every pleasure and every pain, every error and every making straight, all truth in myth and every falsehood of history, the small sin, the great sacrifice, – tales of witch, goblin, and fairy, the record of brave battles and cruel defeat, of victory and renunciation, of oppression suffered and freedom won, to warm a man's heart with his father's memories, and to show him, if he would see them, the hands drawn upward out of this medley of his passion, in search of the new thing which brings harmony out of discord, and lovely reason into the broken tale of a fool.

Some say that before he died the builder saw in very stone his Temple of Joy; others say he died in great content, having found that for which he only imagined the great shrine would resemble.

But all agree that over his tomb were carved these words of his making:

"He who seeks pleasure eats burnt bread. But he who finds Joy has all pleasure in his pocket."

Publisher's Postscript

The preceding first and last chapters of *The Laughing Elf* were edited for modern readers. Ronald's style in this fable and for the dialog in his historical novels was to imitate 17th century authors for effect. However, his publisher for *Sword of the King* in 1900 thought the archaic sentence structure was sometimes confusing. Ronald defended his style in a letter:

> I would rather not lose the slightly quaint effect, I think." [...]
> "The five passages you mention for simplification do not appear to me to need it. I hardly like to appear pig-headed about my work, but I have spent so many months of time and thought over the construction of a uniform style, that I am unwilling to lose the occasional touch of a complexity that falls, I believe, very far short of that to be found in my models. If I began to alter it now I should have to carry the principle throughout, and I fear should lose a good deal of the flavour which is what I chiefly prize in the book.

The Laughing Elf was difficult to understand due it's "quaint" language and complex sentence structure. Parts of it were nearly incomprehensible. Ronald eventually revised some of his archaic language for *Sword of the King* as is shown in another letter to his publisher dated sixteen days after the letter quoted above. He wrote:

> I should like to have a revise, as one or two of my little archaisms seem to have puzzled the compositors.

Although I was reluctant to alter the original text, it more important for readers to understand his message, clear evidence of Ronald's ability to come to terms with the personal difficulties conveyed in Dale Slusser's reconstruction of his life in America.

Robert Trexler, publisher

Appendix E
GEORGE MACDONALD: A Personal Note

by Ronald MacDonald
Preface by Dale Wayne Slusser

The following essay is a reprint of a biographical essay, "George MacDonald: A Personal Note." written by Ronald for the book: *From a Northern Window: Papers, Critical, Historical and Imaginative.* edited by Frederick Watson & Ian Maclaren, pages 55-113: published by James Nisbet in 1911. Ronald was 51 years old when he penned this loving portrait of his father.

Sunrise Books published a new edition of the essay in 1989 as Volume 1 of their *Masterline Series.* Having gone out of print, we again present this touching essay of Ronald's as not only evidence of Ronald's own skill as a writer, but more importantly as evidence of the loving relationship between father and son. The love, respect and admiration of the son for his father shines radiantly in this short biographical tribute to George MacDonald.

Re-reading the essay I was reminded of a short note that I found which Ronald had written to his sister Winifred, a year later (1912), on the occasion of the anniversary of George MacDonald's birthday. The note simply read:

"I just want to send you my love on Father's birthday. Every time I think of him, he grows, it seems, greater and closer. Perhaps that is what he's doing – who knows."

GEORGE MACDONALD: A Personal Note

by Ronald MacDonald

George MacDonald often expressed his wish that no biography of him should be written. His books contained all that he had to say to the world, and the rest did not matter. Modesty and a keen perception of the insincerity and impertinence of books written about men's lives, so soon after the breath is out of their bodies as may be commercially convenient, had perhaps their share in this desire for silence; but it seems probable that there was also a subtler and stronger reason.

For, while in his genial and catholic humanity he took full pleasure in the approbation and sympathetic appreciation of every honest man, woman and child with whom he came in personal contact, he seemed to care nothing for that collective praise which we call fame; and yet knew himself, although I think he never used such a phrase, for a man with a mission. To which point, as being essential to the understanding of the work which is the highest and almost complete expression of his character, I shall return.

To be known by his fruits, then, was not only, if that mattered, the best, way to be known; it was the way also by which any man seeking to know him must come again and again in contact with that something greater than George MacDonald which was the coefficient of his greatness.

He was, perhaps, too careless of himself, and too consistently trustful of others, to dread the quaint perversions and distortions of the ordinary biographer; but, even as his message was larger than himself, he was perhaps not unwilling that curiosity in search of the less should run the sacred risk of being caught by the greater.

It is not without a certain shrinking, in sight, as it were, of so simple and modest a character, that I make use of the words *mission* and *message*. Association has begun to corrupt at least their good odour. Hypocrisy and egoism have not availed, it is true, to damage the plain significance of two honest and useful words. But some of us have come, by a habit of caution forced upon us, to suspect either egoism or hypocrisy in the man that declares himself a messenger or missionary; and in this case it is not hypocrisy which has done the more harm, for hypocrisy is generally logical enough. But who does not know and shrink from the missionary, swollen with the vanity of egoism, and mistaking it, if at first for an ideal pregnancy, yet finally and inevitably for a spiritual parthenogenesis? The man whose every, word and action in pursuit of his glorified hobby claims for himself a mission, even while he cannot be said to have forgotten the *sender* he never knew, is perhaps a very modern type. But he takes a part, with other forms of ignorance and folly, in debasing a great tongue, and in driving sincerity and simplicity in search of new terms for which the dictionaries show no need.

George MacDonald, I repeat, in speaking of himself and his work, said nothing of *mission* nor of *message*. But to carry once more the news which grows greater with age, to carry it with the freshness and new brilliance that come from the mouth of a new poet to his own and succeeding generations, was none the less the moving principle of his life. And to this purpose may be traced not only the lofty form of his verse and his imaginative prose, but even the defects of his more prosaic novels.

These are the expression to his known, wider and inferior public of that same truth which those, in form more enduring for its beauty, offer to the race.

Before leaving this matter of the biography which George MacDonald held unnecessary for the world and distasteful to himself, it is worth pointing out that there is an aspect of his statement that his printed words are sufficient, which he himself would have been slow to perceive; but which, nevertheless, should be of the last consolation to those who, in their affection for the man or admiration of his work, might desire the record of his life to be written down in detail. It is this: that there has probably never been a writer whose work was a better expression of his personal character. This I am not engaged to prove; but I very positively assert from knowledge, that in his novels, his fantastic tales and allegories, and most vividly, perhaps, in his verse, one encounters, or rather lives with, the same rich imagination, the same generous lover of God and man, the same consistent practiser of his own preaching, the same tender charity to the sinner with the same uncompromising hostility to the sin, which were known in daily use and by his own people counted upon more surely than sunshine.

The ideals of his didactic novels were the motive of his own life. In view of some recent controversy, there comes to me almost the temptation to commit the indiscretion of proving, step by step, and point by point, that we have had until lately a poet, known very widely as a preacher, as well as for his religious and ethical writings, living among us a life of literal, and, which is more, imaginative consistency with his doctrine.

George MacDonald was born in the last month of the year 1824, in the small town of Huntly in Aberdeenshire. More than fifty years later, thinking not at all, I must suppose, of himself, he wrote, in the fortieth chapter of *The Marquis of Lossie*, the following words:

> "Rare as they are at any given time, there have been,
> I think, such youths in all the ages of the world-youths
> capable of glorying in the fountain whence issues the
> torrent of their youthful might."

I quote the passage, which has explicit reference to the leading character of the novel in which it occurs, because just such a youth do I imagine the man who wrote it to have been. If such he was, of such he surely remained. Comparison of the best of his early work and the best of his latest will demonstrate truth of the assertion, so far as his mind and purpose are concerned; for the way in which he lived the thing he taught, those who did not know him personally must, in any case, depend upon the witness of those who did. Let them find two voices.

His first printed work was a dramatic poem, entitled *Within and Without*, published in 1855, but written, I believe, in the late forties. In this drama of a man's soul are embedded many lyrics, two of which at least I hold equal in both perfection of form and maturity of feeling to any of his later work. The first of these of poems[142] is so full of beauties

---

132 "Love me, beloved, &c.," vol. i. pp. 79, 80, *Poetical Works of George Macdonald*, 2 vols. Chatto & Windus.

that I had intended quoting from it enough to suggest the depth, tenderness, and yet the serenity of the human passion with its divine foundation which it expresses, but refrain because I cannot quote the whole.

The second[143] is the lament of an orphan child for her parents, and second to nothing of its kind, I think, in the language; its pathos is common to the whole race, and the music of its simplicity attainable only by the finished craftsman that is also poet born. But not even of this will I quote less than the whole.

To these two poems I refer, however, that any who cares to follow the reference may see for himself not only that the poet was there in the beginning, not only that the craftsman was adept in early life, but that the motive thought for which the man became afterwards famous as novelist, preacher, lecturer, and friend, from the earliest days of his writing at least, as sure and powerful as in his latest little Christmas poem to his friends.

This book was followed by his first volume of shorter poems; and then came *Phantastes*, that prose poem whose luxuriance of fancy never once. obscures the profundity of its spiritual imagination. As this was his third book, so was *Lilith* his last but one. And *Lilith* is to *Phantastes* as the old man to the young; but the same man—the same great thought—the same wide hope, and the same rare poet—to adapt his own words quoted above—glorying in the fountain of his youthful might.

Phantastes, published in 1858, uses for its machinery of mystery the primaeval fairy-tale and the mediaeval romance; *Lilith*, in 1895, the mythology of the Talmud and the romance of the fourth dimension of space.

In each case, however, the *passing out* thus procured is but a quaint introduction to that country which every man has within himself; though many, it seems, never find it; while of those who do find, most are led to the great discovery by the guiding hand of a poet.

It is the land where the relation of truth and beauty is easily explained in the vernacular; the land where the life lost for love is found in glory; the land where love is the reward love, and never its price. The

---

133 "Once I was a child, &c.," ibid., pp. 66,67.

land of no bargains, where the *ego* reaches its apotheosis something better than Nirvana.

From boyhood to old age, I must believe, George MacDonald had the freedom of that country; was fluent and scholarly in its speech as in our own; passed freely, it seems, from it to us, from us to it; but, if one may attempt translating a smatter of its tongue, lived in it most freely while his presence was most vivid among us others. The guidance of pilgrims to this land of faerie, as he loved writing the old word, was his business; of his pilgrims, some never left it, some journeyed to and fro, and some keep only dream-like memories of what he there showed them.

But never did he say the land was of his making; never did he speak of its light as shining more for him or his than for any other man that cometh into the world. He was but one of those who knew the way.

> "Better to sit at the water's birth
> Than a sea of waves to win ;
> To live in the love that floweth forth,
> Than the love that cometh in."[144]

This is the spirit of *Lilith* in 1895, as it was of *Phantastes* in 1858.

In varying degree every poet, whether of pen, brush, or chisel, gives such guidance. But I am concerned here to show, or, at least, declare, that this one held fast the intent of opening, if it were never so little, the eyes of his fellows to the vision of the unseen; and to this inflexible continuity of purpose he owed, doubtless, many an adverse contemporary criticism.

In *Blackwood's Magazine* for March 1891 there appeared an article by the late Sir William Geddes, entitled" George MacDonald as a Poet." The rank claimed in the sacred order is high; the argument good, so far as it goes; while the quoted evidence supports the main contention only less strongly than a wider knowledge of the poems, or, perhaps, a less narrow taste, might have done.

> " ...justice compels the conclusion that, after the Laureate,
> there is one, and we fear only one, whose claim stands out
> pre-eminent for this Orphic crown."

---

144 *Phantastes*, 1st ed., chap. xix. p. 243.

"And yet a poet he is by nature and the grace of God; he is a prose writer and novelist only in the second resort, by what we deem an evil fate, the compulsion of 'the Row' and the yoke of the publishers, who have too long bound him in shackles as their slave …and we even make bold to say that in native gift of poetic insight he was born with a richer dower than has fallen to any of our age since Alfred Tennyson saw the light of day."

"To have the dew of one's youth retained under the browner shades of life or beneath the snows of age, to be one of those whose heart has kept pure the holy forms of young imagination, is the prerogative of genius; and to none has this special phase of that prerogative been given in our age more largely than to George MacDonald."

In another passage, Sir William Geddes modestly opines that his poet may have been led to a "withdrawal from his first allegiance," by "the desire to influence opinion theologically as a preacher rather than as a poet, and hence may have suggested itself, as a vehicle for theological views, the prose fiction, to which he has given so much of his strength and power."

I have quoted thus much from the article in *Blackwood* for several reasons: because it is signed, because it was contemporary, because it was written by a Scot, a scholar, and a gentleman, and because it is typical of the better kind of critical misapprehension of the man and of the work which from the beginning he had set himself to do, and in the end had done with a completeness seldom, I believe, surpassed. And I prefer, very naturally, to take for my critic to be refuted one with the merit of rating so high George MacDonald's performance in the nobler literary branch of his writing. That Sir William Geddes should cite in support of his high contention by no means the highest evidence to be found in George MacDonald's verse hurts neither his argument nor mine. His is this: that George MacDonald was a poet who harmed his poetic achievement by deserting his Muse. Mine is, that George MacDonald was one of the endless chain of the interpreters of God to man; that, never losing sight of his privilege and duty of interpretation, he would, all his life, use the best means in his reach and judgment to achieve each separate stage of his over-ruling purpose. Might one imagine him in the simile of a water-fowl, one would say that flying , was his joy, but swimming often walking sometimes his simple duty, when his finny fellows or his pedestrian brothers were the holy quarry.

None that had seen his untiring use, during the preparation of some new edition, of the *ultima lima*—until lovers of the old, not always without reason, have prayed him to have done with polishing —could doubt that verse was the mistress of his poetical passion. But one that has read him through in book, that has seen him laugh and weep, and heard him praise and blame; that has sat at table with him, served him and been served by him; that has heard him read, lecture, preach, and argue, knows that the mistress of poetical form was at any hour deserted upon the slightest summons of a certain master; to be sought again at leisure, and found making pretence that she had not all the while been following, close, but a little behind, to lend the tenderest touches even to the least famous and most pedestrian of his religious romances.[145]

Once I asked him why he did for change and variety, write a story of mere human passion and artistic plot. He replied, that he would like to write it. I asked him then further whether his highest literary quality was not in a measure injured by what must to many seem the monotony of his theme-referring to the novels alone. He admitted that this was possible; and went on to tell me that, having begun to do his work as a Congregational minister, and having been driven, by causes here inconvenient to be stated, into giving up that professional pulpit,[146] he was no less impelled than compelled to use unceasingly the new platform whence he had found that his voice could carry so far.

Through stories of everyday Scottish and English life, whose plot, consisting in the conflict of a stereotyped theology with the simple human aspiration towards the divine, illustrated the solvent power of orthodox Christianity, he found himself touching the hearts and stimulating the consciences of a congregation never to be herded in the largest and most comfortable of Bethels.

---

145 *Mary Marston.* e.g., and *Home Again* are for all their beauty in certain passages and characters, the *applied mechanics* of his theory – what I have called above *religious romances. Phantastes* and *Lilith* are spiritual romances; to the higher mind, of a religious influence far loftier.

146 *Vide passim, Paul Faber,* chap. xxviii. I have no reason to think that any character occurring in the passage is in any sense a portrait; I am sure the episode is invented. But I judge it, from internal evidence alone, to be typical.

His highest form of appeal he never neglected; from writing verse you could not have withheld him so easily as from drawing breath. But at his wider if more ephemeral means of his kind to wisdom he worked with an industry and cordiality which many a good craftsman would thank God to have at his daily command.

In a literary life of some forty-two (to count from the publication of his first book to that of his last) George MacDonald produced some fifty-two volumes; of which twenty-five may be classed as novels, three as prose fantasies, eight as tales and allegories for children, five as sermons, three as literary and miscellaneous critical essays, and three as collections short stories; and five volumes of verse, the greater part of which, with many poems gathered from the pages of the prose works, arranged in two volumes and finally revised by his own hand, was reissued in 1893. But the volume of those two volumes, the versatility of that verse, the variety of its unity, the spiritual insight, the high poetic expression and the exquisite workmanship, make them, in my thinking, the enduring work of his life. He did the work had set himself, one might say, twice over; once, in divers forms and with varying skill, that he who had not the leisure or the learning to read the higher tongue might catch the word hot from wise lips, or fresh in the plain tale of a daily life which he could understand; and again, alternating the more lovely and endurable work with the ephemeral, he left us a legacy of poetry enshrined in verse to bear witness of his witnessing so long as this language, the quest of the divine and the love of beauty shall endure.

This in itself, I think, is a great day's work; and it was accomplished under the strain of a very large family of his own and another of his adoption; it was combined with the periodical delivery of lectures upon Shakespeare, Dante, Browning, Tennyson, and who not else; with the editorship for some years of a magazine (not the least of labours to that just and scrupulous mind); while his Sundays in many years were filled with preaching from the pulpits of any who might invite him. After his abandonment of the predicant profession, he never took remuneration for a spoken sermon; and never, I am sure, refused his preaching, from whatever Christian denomination the invitation might come. I remember very well his saying that the Unitarians were among the most instant to get him to preach; and that he always stipulated for liberty to maintain the doctrine of the Trinity; by which orthodoxy I do not think he ever gained a Sunday's rest.

Should I to all this attempt adding what I know of his private counsel to the anxious and doubting in those matters which he thought of first importance, or to those with a fine point of casuistry weighing upon an awkward and perhaps not seldom a hypertrophied conscience, I should in certain quarters, I believe, be laughed at for the smallness of my knowledge

And yet, throughout the greater part of his working life, his health was bad. There is many an early memory still with me of determined risings from bed (it seems as if those were always days of the old fashioned fog and the straw-carpeted four-wheel cab) to go half or quite across London to preach or lecture to some outlying band of suburban intellectuals, or unknown gathering of sectaries; and if his lecture was often a noble kind of sermon, his sermon had always the high quality of inductive reasoning to support a very moving *ex tempore* eloquence.

This, then, is my plea, or defense, or declaration of belief, If critics have pointed, or shall point to inequality in George MacDonald's work; if they shall say, as they have said, why not this kind only, which is so good, and why so much of that, which is not so good? I reply that his best would not have been the good that it is, if he had been other than the man he was-the man to whom no time was less than eternal in its moment, no crowd composed of men not his brothers in need. For the sake of his best was he to refuse them what here and now was their best? That he would do, and not leave this undone. So to his day he gave sermons, from his own pages and other men's pulpits. And he left to us also of his very best in form and inspiration a bulk of which I do not think the one critic I have quoted had any idea.

But here I would qualify the use which I have made above of the word *ephemeral*. It was adopted advisedly, because the theological, ecclesiastical, and ethical problems of today are as evanescent in form as the need of such controversy is constant in the nature of man. The prophet who has spent years in telling slaves that the Creator is no cruel tyrant to punish senselessly, might, had he lived another decade, be telling them, from the same heart and brain, that He will pass over nothing. I have heard that George MacDonald said in an *ex tempore* [147]sermon that God is easily pleased, but very hard to satisfy. This balance runs through all his utterance on the subject. Yet he was at one time known most widely for his fight against the Calvinistic doctrines of election and eternity of punishment. Today I think he might be

147 I know of only one occasion upon which he delivered a written sermon.

pained to see how base a sense of freedom from obligation has arisen as a by-product of a religious movement in which he took so influential a part.

I would not, however, be taken to mean that the work to which I have applied the word *ephemeral* is dead; for there is abundant evidence not only that the more vigorous of the Scottish novels and all the fairy tales have a perennial public, but also that there is a personal George MacDonald tradition healthily active. I cannot tell how strangely, I cannot remember how often, in train, steamship, club, hotel, theatre or drawing room I have encountered some flash of a smile, some reminiscent anecdote, some kindness, or some quaint proof of a newer generation's almost personal affection for the man known only from Robert Falconer filtered perhaps through a parent, or *At the Back North Wind*, read or listened to many years ago. The oddest occurrence of this kind will hardly bear repetition in this place; but it showed a man turning, at least for a moment, from a grossness of thought and conversation even more foolish than wicked, to speak eagerly, with a face that shone, of his mother's love and reverence for the man she had never seen.

This tradition, keeping alive the issue and the reading of the more notable prose, makes it impossible to set a limit to George MacDonald's day as didactic preacher.

But, as poet, he will, I believe, hit the future, however it may pride itself on independence of tradition, where his blow will tell.

I say again: he did his work twice, and twice it was well done.

So firmly do I believe that the man himself is more truly represented to us in his work than by any possible attempt at biographical portraiture, that I hesitate to descend into personalities even the most reverent; not only because he himself heartily hated the gossiping foolishness, even when kindly, of the biography-makers, but also because anecdote and characteristic episode, however descriptive to the narrator, are liable to strangest perversion of bearing, when wrenched from the full context of life.

Yet, in spite of such risk and a natural diffidence, I am tempted by stronger considerations into sketching an outline of George MacDonald's person and intimate character.

In my earliest memory he was a man of forty; tall, with the build of an athlete, narrow-flanked and broad-shouldered; the hands and feet long and very finely formed; a head with brows and nose of great power; the hair and full beard as black as I have seen where there was no sheen of blue in it; and the eyes, rather deep-set, of a blue liquid as southern sea-water at rest, keen as a northern sky in cloudless frost at mid-day—the only eyes I have known with always a spark and sometimes a flash in them.

The weakness of his lungs in early manhood, and the frequent asthma and bronchitis from which he suffered throughout middle age, rendered him, with the medical notions of fifty and sixty years ago, of very sedentary habit. But I have heard that before my knowledge of him he was fond of boxing, a very quick hitter and clever with the gloves. His great outdoor pleasure was to be in the saddle. He had an excellent seat, and an almost passionate love of horses, and, as his readers know, a very charming and convincing touch in their description. To my mind at this moment from the pages of his novels come five or six horses at least, each with a personality clearly marked. Of these the delightfully melodramatic Kelpie of *The Marquis of Lossie* is perhaps the best known. The gentle, half-Arab Lilith of *Wilfred Cumbermede* may be almost forgotten, but the Lady and the Beelzebub of *St. George and St. Michael*, each with a character well defined as any of the men and women of that delightful romance, have, I think, a long life before them.

In an earlier story, *Adela Cathcart*, there is the description of a mare with which, I know from his own mouth, the author was well acquainted: he had himself, I think, ridden her—perhaps to hounds; and her feat of crossing the railway cutting, described in chapter xix., was local history. His picture of this animal is worth quoting as a model in its kind:—

> "In fact, she was a thoroughgoing hunter; no beauty, certainly, with her ewe-neck, drooping tail, and white face and stocking; but she had an eye at once gentle and wild as that of a savage angel, if my reader will condescend to dream for a moment of such an anomaly; while her hind-quarters were power itself, and her fore-leg was flung right out from the shoulder with a gesture not of work but of delight; the step itself entirely one of work—long in proportion to its height. The lines of her fore and hind

quarters converged so much, that there was hardly room for more than the saddle between them. I had never seen such action. Altogether, although not much of a hunting man, the motion of the creature gave me such a sense of power and joy, that I longed to be scouring the fields with her under me."

This picture of one of his friends has seemed best worth quoting. But there are few of his novels where you will not find a horse; if only appearing as a property and not as a character, its presence will yet be touched with knowledge and tenderness.

In George MacDonald's blood the Gael at least preponderated very largely; and I cannot doubt that the tradition which existed in his family of escape from the Glencoe massacre affected his imagination strongly, giving him a heart equally open to the Highland and the Lowland appeal.

In the main it is the Saxon Scot, whom from childhood he best knew, that he shows us in the best of his novels; but his occasional picture of a Highlander will stand out from the canvas with great distinction; and it may be doubted whether he ever equaled in clarity of characterization or profundity of loving humour his Duncan MacPhail, the blind piper of Portlossie.[148]   In his lofty, yet half savage sense of honour, his feminine tenderness, his berserk fits of rage, his jubilant piping, his love of personal finery undimmed by blindness, and in the poetic imagery of his speech; in his noble lament for Glencoe and his terrible cursing of Campbells; in his chivalrous worship of all women and his bitter hatred of one, Duncan, who must in the end confess himself a MacDonald, is at once the type of the Celt for his author, and the reconstruction (I suggest merely) of the influence upon his author of Highland tradition. Much that Duncan relates of Glencoe and Culloden, as well as certain passages in Robert Falconer concerning the "blin' piper o' Portcloddie," is family history—or tradition of that quality which is of more influence upon young minds than fixed record.

Although all hatreds had died out; although George MacDonald's working life was almost entirely spent outside Scotland, and very little of its whole course, I believe, in the Highlands proper; although his scholarly taste led him chiefly to work upon and admire the literature

---

148 *Malcolm*

of England from Langland to Wordsworth, he was, I think, in habit of mind, and in swift brilliance of fancy, radically a Gael. One small but very significant quality in this connection—a quality for which he would often make fun of himself—was his love of finery; a love as keen, I truly believe, and as personal, as old Duncan's. To childish eyes—perhaps to others—George MacDonald was a very splendid sight in full Highland costume; and carried himself in it, upon his rare occasions, with the port that will make the best of a good thing. And yet, whether it were the kilt at a familiar festivity, a new jewel, or some specially gorgeous smoking-jacket or cap, his was always the pleasant pride of perennial childhood; it was, "Please look at my new shoes," rather than, "Look at me because my shoes are new."

He had small peculiarities in dress which became part of his personality; waistcoats made always with some twenty small buttons, often gilt, from collar to waist, of which only the highest, beneath his beard, and the four or five lowest were ever fastened over the soft-fronted white shirt. And for choice, at home, the jacket would be brown or black velvet; while in boots, shoes, and socks he was the gentlest but most persistent of the dandies I have known.

In later years, when the beard and hair were white, in the bright Italian days, and even the better hours of an English summer, a complete suit of white serge or flannel pleased him only less than it pleased his own people.

In precious stones he took a delight almost barbaric, but enriched by the knowledge of the amateur. There is a passage in chapter lxi. of *Castle Warlock* which I will quote as expressing, with a beauty equal at least to its subject, the joy he could take from the light and colour of diamonds.

It describes the pouring out, into a patch of evening sunlight upon a bare floor, of a great treasure-trove of unset precious stones.

> "Into the pool began to tumble a small cataract of shredded rainbows, flashing all the colours visible to the human eye—and more."

When the receptacle is empty,

> "The stream that flowed from it had not spread and sunk and vanished. Based and heaped it lay where it fell, a silent, motionless tempest of conflicting yet utterly harmonious

hues, with a foamy spray of spiky flashes, and spots that ate into the eyes with their fierce colours. In every direction shot from it blinding rays. It was a cairn of diamonds, of all the shapes into which diamonds are fashioned. Ah, the splendrous show of deep-hued, burning, flashing, stinging light! the heaviest of its colours borne light as those of a foam-bubble on the strength of its triumphing radiance. There pulsed the mystical, glowing red—heart and lord of colour; there the jubilant yellow—light crowned to ethereal gold; there the wide-eyed, spirit blue- the truth unfathomable; there the green that haunts the brain— store-land of nature's boundless secrets!—all together striving, yet atoning, fighting and fleeing and following, parting and blending, an illimitable play of infinite force and endlessly delicate gradation. All the gems were there - sapphires, emeralds, and rubies; but they were scarce to be noted in the glorious mass of new-born, ever-dying colour that gushed from the fountains of the light-dividing diamonds."

George MacDonald was a man beyond the ordinary deft with his fingers, and fond of practicing the arts they were master of. A good practical carpenter, a workman-like stitcher of leather, with some practical experience, I fancy, in boyhood, of smith's, or at least farrier's work, his chief pleasure in this kind during his later years was book-binding; its final phase with him being delicate and loving work in the repair of old books. In one of his later novels, *There and Back*, there is much space given to this gentle art of *book-healing*, as he calls it; letting us into the secret of the author's love and reverence for the bodies of his books, and its source in a deeper love of their spirit.

I do not know in how many crafts he may have obtained, at one time or another of his life, some practical experience; but I do know that it would be hard to count those of which he has written incidentally, with knowledge and love that prove his possession of the craftsman's hand and brain, as well as the poet's joy in making things. His tale of *Gutta Percha Willie*, though not in the first rank of his stories for children, convinces the mature reader at least that the writer would take in the simplest of Willie's mechanical contrivances a pleasure second to that of no boy of them all.

The painstaking reverence with which, in St. *George and St. Michael*, he has introduced to the general reader the genius of the second Marquis of Worcester, is further proof of his pleasure in the skill of inventors and their coaxing of natural forces to their ends. At no time, so far as my knowledge goes, did he show a sign of that jealousy of change worked in our lives by mechanical advance which is so natural in the middle-aged and the old. For all his strong historic sense, for all his worship of beauty in tradition and in the monuments of letters and other art, I never heard him use the tone of the *laudator temporis acti*. He was among the first of literary men, I believe, to make use of the typing-machine; the bulk of his work, from the year 1880, being composed by this means, and worked upon afterwards with the pen; he always cheerfully accounting the machine a great saving of labour.

For a man who in the last twenty years of his life went so seldom out of his own house and circle, his interest in all things which men do was surprisingly wide.

If he was one of the best talkers I have known, he was certainly the best of all the listeners. Every fresh man or woman, I used to think, he believed come to him with some new thing. He thought every man was teaching him-even when one did but hand him back his own gift.

In argument he was scrupulously just; and never was man readier to admit his own error or ignorance.

His anger was fulgurous-a Highlander's; but, in my experience, rare, and never for wrong done to himself. Himself the perfection of courtesy, he has confessed to me that the contingency in which he most feared for his self-control was to find himself the object of discourtesy which he believed intentional. Of courtesy received he had a quaint anecdote which, for its comical sweetness, he enjoyed anew every time he told it :

> In the days of the knife-board omnibus, more dead than the stage-coach or the knife-board itself, he trod, in entering the straw-carpeted body of the lumbering caravan, upon the foot of an old woman with, I imagine, large basket and peppermint drops to match. To his apology she replied, smiling: "Use yer freedom, sir-use yer freedom."[149]

---

149 *The Taming of the Shrew*, act v. sc. ii. 1. 179.

Though he could not, I know the grace and tenderness with which her pardon had been asked; and find, consequently, less humour and more feminine human nature than he in her form of acknowledgment.

Notwithstanding his love of childhood, and his readiness upon paper with fanciful combinations hovering round and finally focused in imaginative truth, he was never, until his writing days were done, a *viva voce* story-teller. He has indeed one grandchild who remembers a long, never written, and never finished fairy-tale from his lips; but that was in the days when typing-machine and pen had done their work.

Upon fit occasion he would read aloud, in his strong, musical voice, from which the Scottish inflection had disappeared, although nationality persisted in the quality of the vowels and the richness of the r's, any good stuff suggested to him, provided always it was not from his own books. Very occasionally I have known him, under pressure, read a little from his own verse, but only once, to an invalid, from his prose; upon which last occasion there was a hurried reluctance of delivery unjust to both author and reader.

If he had not been what he was, I would have seen him chief of a clan. The patriarchal idea was in his blood. His own family of eleven children, whatever the narrowness accommodation or banking-account, seemed never enough to keep the house comfortably full. During his lecturing tour in the United States, in 1872-3, it was widely reported that he was father of thirteen children—a mistake proved to be due to his frequent statement that he had "the wrong side of a dozen."

I have no space, and perhaps too much reverence, to pile up here story upon story of this man's good deeds, his kindly acts, and of his sudden sympathetic apprehension, swift as the flash from the blue of the eyes, which never, I believe, launched a bolt not generous, and seldom one not kindly.

Thrice, in a halting attempt to put him upon paper, have I been reminded of his mode of explaining τό πῦρ τό αἰώνιον as simply a manifestation of the love of God—destroying its evil to the salvation of every soul; and each time have I thought of his eyes as they were wont to look at me—sometimes, though these times were a small proportion, not with present comfort.

His personal influence was founded, I think, largely upon the keen interest he showed in any man's tale of himself, and upon his characteristic habit of expecting and believing the best of every man until he knew the contrary; and when I consider the scope of his friendship and acquaintance, it seems not a little wonderful how seldom he was imposed upon.

If he did not love all men, it is a grievous charge against some. That he could love his enemy I am sure as that, in the proper circumstances of human strife, he could have killed his friend without stain of conscience.[150]

Civically and socially men have been contemptible, yet left great work. Great as I think this man's work, I set his conduct of life relatively even higher.

The permanence of his tastes, even of his mere likings and dislikings, gives quaint support to my statement that he had early chosen his course, and spent his time here in following it ; and not, as so many even of the great have done, in digging up his roots to find fresh soil and new nourishment for them. If he could read this he would say, smiling, that he was planted early where the ground was richest.

Bred in a land of religious division, his whole fight was against schism.

Although full of the highest zeal for personal religion, he hated, as a designation, the word *Protestant*. You cannot, he would say, make a belief out of a denial. I could here enlarge curiously upon some effects of his detestation of the disruptive principle which, in the nature of things, is so powerful in the Protestant bodies. But strife, except against a common enemy, was hateful to him. If stumbling-blocks there must be to George MacDonald's weak brother even from George MacDonald himself, let the weak find them in the many pages of the strong on—not in my few.

For a brief period, dating from the end of his course at the University of Aberdeen, he had intended going to Germany to study chemistry in the best school then existing.

---

150 I am reminded of a passage in chapter viii. of *St. George and St. Michael*: ". ..beware of private quarrel in such a season of strife. This youth and thyself may meet...on the battlefield; and ...in such case I would rather slay my friend than my enemy."

In many of his novels and even other writings we find the poet's interest in natural science, with traces here and there of a technical knowledge which, if it could not keep pace in practical detail with the seven-leagued strides of discovery, yet enabled him to follow with keen interest the theories and philosophical tendency of modern scientific thought. And I believe that to the end science did but give him fresh pasture for an insatiable and fearlessly religious imagination.

By the pen of a great prose-writer, whose fame sprang first in other fields, we have been offered in the last quarter of a century the interpretation of certain ethical and spiritual aspects of Christianity, detached from traditional sanction. These, in the more Western civilizations at least, have been most influential with those who may be called, with technical accuracy, the unbelievers.

George MacDonald, at an earlier date, was in the prime of his great effort to revive personal religion within the fold. He made no war upon the Church as he knew it—whether Independent, Presbyterian, or Anglican; his war was upon the faithlessness of the officially faithful, and, incidentally only, upon one or at two Calvinistic and Augustinian dogmas exaggerated out of all proportion to their service.

If it were not that George MacDonald will always (nor to me alone) make his individuality felt between the lines—between even adjective and substantive, subject and predicate—I would that say that now I have done with both his person and his personality. Since that is too much to promise, let me proceed to consider, as much apart from its writer as may be, his work.

He was a great reader, of wide, and, in some subjects, profound erudition. His knowledge of English poetry from Chaucer to Browning surpassed that of any other man whose knowledge I have known. His familiarity with the thought and writings of William Law, Henry More, George Fox, Blake, Swedenborg, Behmen and Jean Paul Richter—and I know not what other mystics—implies an amount of study for which how he found the time is a wonder to me; he had both the scholar's and the poet's mastery of Milton, Shakespeare, and Dante; he read his Germans, his Frenchmen, and his Italians in their own words; had read the New Testament at least (with which he would always begin his attack upon a new language) in Dutch, modern Greek, and, I think, Spanish, and knew it best, I am sure, in its oldest tongue. To classical scholarship he laid little claim; but I have heard him read Horace aloud so that the lines lived and swung with the poetry which had till then been more dead to me than their tongue or even their commentators.

Russian novelists he always read through their French translators, and advised this medium to others.

Of the translator's duty he supported the severest standard, characteristically applying it to himself in the extreme. I have heard him say, speaking more especially of German verse, that it was not translated until not only the sense and the metre were rendered, but even the rhymes. This finish I believe he succeeded to a great extent in giving to his English versions of Novalis and others. And here I cannot refrain from quoting what is, I think, his single translation from Horace—the two last stanzas, namely, of the ode beginning, "Aequam memento rebus in arduis." I do not think the lines are included in his collected verse, but they may be found at the end of the second chapter of *Thomas Wingfold*, presented as the work of the clergyman who gives title to the book:

> " No hair it boots thee whether from Inachus,
> Ancient descended, or of the poorest born,
> Thy being drags all bare and roofless,
> Victim the same of the heartless Orcus.
>
> "All are on one road driven; for each of us
> The urn is tossed, and, later or earlier,
> The lot will drop and all be sentenced
> Into the boat of eternal exile,"

Not George MacDonald's thought; even as rendered, merely the Rev. Mr. Wingfold's sympathetic echo of Q. Horatius Flaccus' gentle despair; but how metrically and dramatically correspondent with:

> " Divesne prisco natus ab Inacho,
> Nil interest, an pauper et infima
> De gente sub divo moreris,
> Victima nil miserantis Orci.
> " Omnes eodem cogimur; omnium
> Versatur urna serius ocius
> Sors exitura, et nos in æternum
> Exsilium impositura cumbae."

I have chosen this specimen of George MacDonald's skilful fidelity as translator, because it is the best of which I can personally judge; I wish I had enough German to show what I am told are the greater beauties to be found in his rendering of Novalis, Goethe, Uhland, Heine, and others, published in 1876 in a small volume entitled *Exotics*; of which the preface, stating George MacDonald's principles of translation, is to me more interesting than any of the poems intrinsically.

Now, since the man who undertakes research into the bibliography, philology, genesis, and motive of a great poem; who makes himself humbly its expositor to those upon whom its beauty has shone through a mist of time and technical ignorance; and who seeks, even in his boldest and least conventional opinions, to clear away rather than to excite doubt and bewilderment, is in very high sense a translator, this is, I think, the point at which I should refer to George MacDonald's greatest achievement of literary interpretation; I mean, his edition of the *Tragedy of Hamlet*, published in the year 1885 by Longmans, Green & Co., and reissued since his death by Arthur Fifield. Upon the title-page it is described as "a study with the text of the Folio of 1623." It is a work of deep insight and high scholarship. Its production was a labour of love extending over many years—six, I think he told me. That it is not widely known and accepted for the weight of its authority is due, perhaps, to George MacDonald's psychological and even metaphysical approach.

By what other road so profoundly human a metaphysician as Hamlet could be reached, it seems impossible to guess; but George MacDonald's philosophical and religious bent being better known than his critical acumen and catholic knowledge of English letters, it may very well be that many a student, in fear of insidious sermonizing, has passed by this masterly analysis of Hamlet's character, and lost enlightenment upon the text such as can only be given by scholarship inspired with imagination.

I do not think any lover of Shakespeare can read without deep interest the long note upon the great soliloquy (pp. 123-125); and in this connection it is worth mention that there are contained in a volume called *Orts*, published in 1882 by Sampson Low & Co., three essays on Shakespearian themes which contain, I believe, with the *Hamlet*, all that remains of George MacDonald's ordered thought upon this limitless subject. For the lectures upon Shakespeare, his plays and his poems, as those upon other subjects only less great, were all, so far as my knowledge goes, delivered *ex tempore*.

One other book falls here to be mentioned in connection with his knowledge of our literature. It may be described as a review of English religious poetry from the thirteenth century down to Keble. The selections are of great richness, the commentary, historical and critical, full of wisdom and sympathy. But the book has its chief value, from our present point of view, in the side-light thrown from it upon the writer's taste, both in his choice, and by what he tells us of the principles upon which he has chosen.[151]

The twenty-five novels fall naturally into two divisions—those of Scottish and those of English life and character.

The Scotch number twelve, of which *Robert Falconer*, *Alec Forbes*, *Malcolm*, and *Sir Gibbie*, in respect of structure, characterization, pathos, and humour stand easily first. In point of time, *David Elginbrod* precedes them all, and throughout its first book (forming, in the dear old three-decker form, two-thirds of the first volume) smells of the earth, of Scotland, and of all humanity as strongly as *Robert Falconer* or *Alec Forbes*. The novel also enshrines one character, as near the sublime as George MacDonald has ever shaped (and that is saying much)—David Elginbrod himself; who, by a very wizard's touch of art, dominates the tale, although we meet him, after that wonderful first book, only in the good that could not be interred with his bones. Throughout the rest of the tale we wander, as did that Scottish tutor, in a land too strange; and long, with him, to get home. Which is where, in the last five pages of the book, we find ourselves—pages as sweet, as human, and of as heavenly a beauty as you will find anywhere in this or another novelist. Nor can it be denied that we have between whiles flashes of the land we have left and are going towards—those passages, I mean, where the black eyes and broad shoulders of Robert Falconer, in the midst of the great life whose great boyhood was yet to be written, seem to heave themselves up through the swamp of London mud, and the man's gaze to pierce clothes, flesh, and bones into what little heart may be ours. And yet the tale, for him that wrote it, is but a preliminary canter. Had I been a man when *David Elginbrod* struggled at last into print, after traditional manuscript adventures, in the year 1863, I should, I think, have read it with a great reverence, but even greater expectation.

---

151 *England's Antiphon*. Macmillan, 1874

In *Alec Forbes*, the second novel, he was well into his stride; in *Robert Falconer*, the third (to maintain a metaphor after his own heart), fully extended.

One may lay his own little fern-leaf upon his choice of a favourite writer's books, yet never claim for it the dignity of the palm. If I were asked to pick out the best of George MacDonald's novels, I should be found hesitating between *Alec Forbes* and *Robert Falconer*. For the first, I should say that the tale, the atmosphere, and the colour are greater than anyone character among the many which go in this book to the making of that one great thing and two great qualities. *Robert Falconer*, on the other hand, is broken by its change of scene; less because change there is, than by the contrast between the author's handling of this picture and that; his small Aberdeenshire town is to me, a Cockney of Scottish descent, historic Scotland—a spot of it only, and even perhaps but a phase of that spot; but both spot and phase are true with the truth which makes the difference between a mere metal ring and the link of a chain. Robert Falconer's London is but a bit of any big town, whose horrors, contrasts, and possibilities are still a stimulating brew to the poet dropped into its caldron perhaps a bare twenty years before. He wrote of it as he saw it in the fifties and sixties; but it is a ring, not a link.

Whether I be right or wrong in discovering a greater homogeneity in *Alec Forbes* than in *Robert Falconer*, few of their readers, I imagine, will differ from me when I say that *Robert Falconer* is the high-water mark of George MacDonald's character drawing. The book contains at least four characters which have seldom been surpassed for truth, vigour, and loving humour: Dooble Sanny, Shargar, Falconer's grandmother, and the great Bob himself. If there be anywhere in modern fiction a figure worthy to set beside his, it is Jean Valjean's.

Even the London drawing-room of the fifties cannot take the salt out of Shargar. When his very wicked but legitimate brother says to him, in presence of a young gentlewoman, "You are either a liar or a bastard, then," the delightful Shargar replies, "No liar, my lord, but a bastard, thank heaven!" A drama epitomized, for him who knows how to expand.

These people of *Robert Falconer* are upon a greater scale than those of *Alec Forbes*, and touched with a hand no less sure than that which gave life to Cupples, Thomas Cran, the Rev. Mr. Cowie, Robert Bruce, and Annie Anderson. I am inclined to think Robert Bruce the most successful male[152] villain of George MacDonald's novels; and surely his claim to distinguished ancestry is among the best of the ironies which stick in the memory. But it is worth noting that *Robert Falconer*, the greater, if less finished book, contains among its younger women none worthy to hold a candle to the Annie of *Alec Forbes*. Her I should know if I met her—but hardly the Mary St. John nor the Mysie Lindsay of *Robert Falconer*.

Their temptations notwithstanding, I am not going to compile a list of George MacDonald's characters drawn most aptly to my taste. Not only would my choice surely run counter to other and equally justifiable opinion, but the tale of them would be too long in the telling. Well as I know his novels, and various as find their merit, I can think of none without one character at least to hold attention in reading, and to remain, as a kind of friend that would be talked with, if met, upon a known basis of previous intimacy. These are all so human to me, that if at times I find in them a common tendency to cleave too closely to a single great subject, I say to myself that for this the poor dears are hardly to be blamed.

Of the English novels, thirteen in number, one only, perhaps, can rank with the best of the Scotch; yet to four others, at least, of the English, I would assign higher place than to the latest six of the Scotch.

The one is *Annals of a Quiet Neighbourhood*; and the four are *Wilfred Cumbermede*, *Thomas Wingfold*, *Paul Faber*, and *St. George and St. Michael*. His handling of English character and conditions grew with the years more sure and more delicate; while the later Scottish books tend increasingly, I think, to paler repetition of the types which glowed with a life so vivid in the earlier.

This is, for what it may be worth, my selection of ten out of the twenty-five novels. Yet no sooner have I written it than I begin to hear soft, inward clamour of the voices appealing against neglect. Sometimes

---

152 To put it very mildly, George MacDonald always gave the benefit of the doubt to the woman. He had, indeed, a very lovable prejudice in the woman's favour. It is therefore remarkable, if my criticism be just, that among those people who may, in crudely technical phrase, be called his villains, the females are artistically much more convincing than the males. I suggest, with all diffidence, that he understood women the better.

it is individual persons, sometimes a dialogue or a description, sometimes a tense situation that cries or whispers for recognition. Characters thus standing out from this secondary rank of tales are chiefly those of women; scarce one of the novels which I have classed below the first rank being without a picture of feminine grace not to be forgotten. A very few among them are in a measure portraits. Now, portraiture was a branch of his art which George MacDonald did not often attempt, and for which I do not think he was especially well fitted; the women and the men moulded afresh from his general knowledge of human nature being, to my thinking, more life-like than the few upon whom he attempted the perilous feat of transplantation from the soil of those circumstances which he could but know in part to that which he must create for them altogether. Yet is it possible that, where the models are unknown, these few characters do not suffer by comparison with the rest; wherefore, so far as I am concerned, unknown they shall remain.

Even from the very last book which he wrote, *Salted with Fire*, a book written with failing powers, of heavy-footed progression, and with little freshness of imagination, there stands out a passage of peculiar beauty—that in which Isy gives her illegitimate child into his father's arms; a little scene so simple, so strong, and so human as to soften, if not wipe out altogether one's tender regret for the author's last gallant effort.

Says to Isy the man who has seduced her, and only now learns his fatherhood:

"Is this mine?"

"Yours and mine, sir," she replied. "Wasna God a heap better to me nor I deserved? Sic a bonnie bairn! No a mark, no a spot upon him frae heid to fut to tell that he had no business to be here! Gie the bonny wee man a kiss, Mr. Blatherwick. Haud him close to ye, sir, and he'll tak the pain oot o' yer hert; aften has he ta'en 't oot o' mine-- only it aye cam again! He's yer ain son, sir! He cam to me bringing the Lord's forgiveness, lang or ever I had the hert to speir for't. Eh, but we maun dee oor best to mak up till God's bairn for the wrang we did him afore he was born! But he'll be like his great Father, and forgie us baith!"

In pondering what may in a few pages be said of George MacDonald's poetry—of the expression in verse, I mean, of that shining imagination by which even an ethical conflict framed in a theological plot is made a drama of the spirit—I find myself impelled, scarce knowing why, to mount the steps of his fairy-tales, and to pass through the hall of entrance where stand *Lilith* and *Phantastes*, one on either hand, like two strange sphinxes, with each its constant form, and each with its ever changing beauty of countenance-sphinxes asking questions which none will regret his endeavour to answer—into that inner shrine of which the architecture is verse and poetry the indwelling spirit.

In 1867 was published a green-and-gold-covered octavo volume called *Dealings with the Fairies;* it holds five tales, explicitly offered to children, of which none, I think, lacks, beneath the play of an exuberant fancy, imaginative suggestion of deeper things. The first three had appeared earlier in a novel called *Adela Cathcart*, wherein the members of a story-telling club criticize freely the tales read aloud to them. One has glimpses among these remarks, censures and defenses, of George MacDonald's own opinion of this part of his work, and of his design in constructing these and certain other tales. If any should be curious enough to follow up this reference, let him do so in the first edition of *Adela Cathcart* (Hurst & Blackett, 3 vols. 1864); for in the reprint in one volume of 1882 many of the short stories have been replaced by others of different quality.

In three out of these five tales it is worth noting with what varying beauty, as in *Lilith* and *Phantastes*, is handled the passage from this known world to that other which George MacDonald makes at least credible.

The last of the five is a complete poetic allegory (or parable, as he preferred calling such work) of his very best, and among the most popular with children. With this (*The Golden Key*) I would class, as his best allegories, *The Princess and the Goblin* and *The History of Photogen and Nycteris*[153]. This last I consider, if not the profoundest, yet certainly the most exquisitely finished, consistently planned, and limpidly written of all his children's fairy-tales. It is also, I think, the last that he wrote. The gentle fancifulness of the word-play by which the idea of "going out," in its spiritual significance, is developed, proceeds in direct line with the unfolding of a story so exciting that children will read and read it times uncounted.

---

153 *The History of Photogen and Nycteris* appeared originally in a volume entitled *Stephen Archer and other Tales.* In a reprint issued by Arthur Fifield, since the author's death, the tale bears the title of *The Day Boy and the Night Girl.*

The Princess and the Goblin, with its cobs, its miners, its lonely garrets above, where yet, with courage, you may find one that is never empty; with its mines where the gold and silver are, and the horrific network of galleries linking the homes of a more terrible people, who fear only the sunlight and the softness of the feet they go upon; with its brave Curdie, who can delve and fight, but must be taught to climb; with its braver princess, learning her way upward so simply (if not without tears) that she can face the terrors of the underworld with a great heart; with that shining thread that will give the reader its name more easily than its touch to his fingers; this story of a princess is a delight and a. wonder, with no limit, in my thinking, to its possible and beautiful interpretations. It is the romance of a poet keeping a childhood more eternal than Peter Pan's—a romance in the terms of all fairy lore; and the work of a sage whose wisdom lay in his poetry.

But *At the Back of the North Wind* is a book of which I cannot write much. It seems to stand, in its mystery and simplicity, with its background of the commonplace, and its abandonment of the tongue and conventions of childish lore, far above its fellows. Here, for child and man alike, George MacDonald gives us the two worlds co-existent; not *here* and *there*, but both here and now. And its three great persons, North Wind, Diamond the boy, and Diamond the cab-horse, speak more wisdom than will ever be spoken about them.[154]

So I come to the adytum—to stand nearly speechless upon its threshold.

The art which does not speak best for itself has little to be said for it; the more perfect in its kind, the more hardly will its meaning be expressed or even hinted at by other words than its own. And yet, to quote from the last paragraph but one of the last chapter but two of *There and Back*[155], "… he held … that the imperfect are the best teachers of the imperfect. … When a man, he said, agonized to get into other hearts the thing dear to his own, the false intellectual and even moral forms in which his Ignorance and the crudity of his understanding compelled him to embody it, would not render its truth of none effect, but might, on the contrary, make its reception possible where a truer presentation would stick fast in the doorway."

---

154 I am reminded that earlier I have relatively disparaged GeorgeMacDonald's London. Yet in this tale London of the late sixties is still vividly alive; because, I suppose, it is seen through those Diamond-eyes.

155 Kegan Paul, Trench, Trübner & Co., 3 vols., 1891.

Upon this authority I will try to write a page or two about the music I cannot even *pianolize* to the reader. But the address of the orchestra which plays it day and night, year in and out, is below. [156]

Cross divisions are the cross of the analyst.

Should I, for practical purposes, begin with a division of his religious verse from his profane, it might be fairly advanced against me that George MacDonald wrote few stanzas and barely a single complete poem which was not of some religious significance.

Should I divide the Scottish from the English verse, I might be asked how should I or any man attempt to base a categorical distinction upon the slight differences between two modern variants of an immemorial tongue.

If I should write of his great knowledge and delightful skill in the variations of English metre, classifying technically according to the types of verse more or less suited to his peculiar genius, I should need no outside critic to show me the risk I ran. For I have not forgotten a discussion between George MacDonald and a minor and younger poet of some sweetness and much facility—a discussion which ended in the elder's frank acknowledgment that his friend knew far more of English prosody than he. It was an occasion—and here digression is in the direction of the high road—upon which I had a single thought—not of prosody, but of the man whose joy it was to find, in whatever region of thought or action, a greater than himself. From horse-shoeing or watch-making up to what I think it would not displease him that I should call spiritual dynamics, there was not the man, left alone with George MacDonald, whose brains he would not pick. He never knew he was picking-and none of his victims have I known that did not think himself in the better of the bargain.

Let us turn, in lack of a system, to his ballads; and first, those in dialect.

If modern has equalled *The Twa Gordons* and *The Auld Fisher*, I wish I knew him. The ironic theology of *The Deil's Forhooit his Ain* is, to say the least, fit to stand with the best of Burns; the very colour of woe and the salt sadness of the sea are in *The Mermaid*; and, for the swinging romance of the attraction in peril of a great woman's heart to a brave man's, give me the virile archaism of *The Yerl o' Waterydeck*.

---

156 *The Poetical Works of George MacDonald*, 2 vols. Chatto & Windus.

In the same music, *The Twa Gordons* goes even deeper into the love of man for man; while *The Mermaid* deals with the love of man for the mystery, haunting every literature, of the semi-human feminine.

The Deifs Forhooit his Ain is the inversion of Christianity-the gospel of despair; the love of nothing, where there is nothing to love:

> "Ye see yon blue thing they ca' the lift?
> It's but hell turn't upside down."

Dixit Diabolus; but hear the refrain of the *Auld Fisher*, in the ballad which covers all the loves, and hopes to find them all in the one:

> "An' it's oh to win awa', awa'!
> An' it's oh to win awa'
> Whaur the bairns come hame an' the wives they bide
> An' God is the father of a' !"

And yet I have but mentioned a very few of the Scottish ballads, and one or two of the loves they sing in the first tongue the singer knew. In it he has sung—sung, and sung, as well as in the English to an even loftier melody, the song of the greatest love of all-the love of God for man; has sung it so variously and nobly that choice of quotation seems impossible. And it is because that song is the first of songs that he will sing all the great songs of the lesser loves so sweetly—because, he might have said in better metaphor, they are all sparks from the anvil of the creating love. Man and horse, dog and man, child and flower, it was all one love for him, from the sunrise of his day to its star-light. I cannot say if there be anywhere a poem without love in it. But very sure I am you will not find me one such of George MacDonald's.

Of the English ballads, *The Legend of the Corrievrechan* is among his few negatives of the theme which cannot grow dull; and it has been called, I have forgotten by what critic of weight, a perfect sampler of the modern ballad.

Abu Midjan, which contains some of the author's finest lyric lines, is the story of the triumph in a Moslem poet of the inspiration of battle over the inspiration of wine, with exquisite songs and a splendid dramatic conclusion. For movement I know few things to equal it.

But first of the English ballads I place *The Thankless Lady* and *The Old Garden*, with the palm certainly to the latter, but for a doubt as to whether the author, its metre notwithstanding, would have called it a ballad at all.

The light touch and the tenderly ironic scheme of *The Thankless Lady*, with its perfect continuity, would turn quotation into vandalism.

But from *The Old Garden*, in its succession of aspects, with each its correlated mood, and at last its heartbreaking suggestion of a tale never told, yet lived again by the maiden ghost, night after eternal night, one may take a little here and there without breaking things.

In early morning:

> "I saw the wise old mansion,
> Like a cow in the noonday heat,
> Stand in a lake of shadows,
> That rippled about its feet."

And, when he has shown us a house of which we seem to remember the beauty, and are peace-fully rejoiced in seeing it again, we are told of her who, unseen but divined,

> "Looked out on the garden dreamy,
> And knew not that it was old;
> Looked past the gray and the sombre,
> And saw but the green and the gold."

In the end, when she has come to the eternal tryst, down a stair which will not creak to her ghostly foot, but only in the ghostly brain, there is no second ghost to meet her.

> "If I cried aloud in the stillness,
> She would never turn her head.
> She is dreaming the sky above her,
> She is dreaming the earth below:-
> This night she lost her lover,
> A hundred years ago."

The poem glides in an ordered progression from aged peace to ghostly desolation of lovelessness; sad and delicate, exquisite in diction, gently vivid in description, and hopelessly forlorn in effect—as if he who could so well tell us what love is, must now and again prove his knowledge by a negative process.

His sonnets, of which there is a great number, both profane and sacred, would in themselves make a long study. To those interested in the workmanship of this lofty and difficult form of verse, and in the subtle variations which its severity permits, George MacDonald's use of it, especially in his handling of the last six verses, with his leaning in later life, I think, to the Shakespearian final couplet, is worth examination. But sonnets, especially sonnets in series, are to be treated even more reverently than ballads.

The Diary of an Old Soul, written, probably, during George MacDonald's fifty-fifth year, privately printed and issued early in 1880, and now published by Arthur Fifield, I can barely describe, and not at all discuss.

It consists in a chain of stanzas, of which the links number three hundred and sixty-six, being one for each possible day in the year. Each link is a stanza of seven verses, of rhymed, five-accent iambic measure, with a wealth of variation in the arrangement of the rhymes, which is extraordinarily effective in averting monotony. The whole is the record of a life's rather than a year's religious thought. So personal, so single-minded, so intense, at once so exalted and profound is this remarkable poem, that criticism of it is only for friends with a common appreciation.

Out of his verse, far greater in quantity than is known even to many of its lovers, there springs to my mind, as typical of his power, versatility, and concentration of design, a poem called *The Haunted House*.

"Suggested," he writes, between its title and first verse, "by a drawing of Thomas Moran, the American painter."

The drawing I know, and the poem; but I do not know the painter that could give me the fleshly horror which this painter's interpreter conveys. For the ghastliness of initial terror Poe might have run Thomas Moran's interpreter close—perhaps equalled him. But hardly, I think, could even Poe, in this the mere mechanism of George MacDonald's idea, have excelled him; for the lurking truth of the horror's spiritual source would have slipped between Poe's fingers; or, perceived, would have been drowned in "damnable iteration."

The growth of dismay in this appalling lyric is hastened by touches of tragic tenderness; until we find that the picture must have still its place upon our wall, because its ghastly moon stares down into the soul that is ours, with a history yet to finish.

Reading it once more, I remember the poet's love for the doctor who spied professionally upon Lady Macbeth. Guessing at the sin behind her agony, he does not pray, "God forgive her," but " God forgive us all!"

More than I had purposed have I dwelt upon the religious aspect of George MacDonald's work; and cannot, indeed, now that I come near an end, see how I could in honesty have done otherwise. For this is not a man with a "religious side" to his nature; nor was he, in my reading of the writer or the written, a "one-sided" man. But the many sides of him shone in one only light; the two lungs breathed one air.

Because his religion was his life, he could no more divide the religious from the secular than a fish separate swimming from water. Whence it came that to religion he gave the cream of his words, spoken and written. In this, like all poets, great or small, his best was said upon the matter which most nearly touched him; and his best was said best in that form of his art towards which he was born with the stronger aptitude, and of which he had early made himself more completely the master.

I have heard of men whose whole lives were coloured by religion. But George MacDonald's life *was* religion; and little, on the other hand, would he thank me for saying that his iridescent imagination gave its colour to the religion that was his. But he will not deny me a measure of insight, if I say that his imaginative faculty was a prism, falling through which the Great White Light was disparted into seventy times seven hues of human delight.

Other Zossima Press Titles

C. S. Lewis

C. S. Lewis: Views From Wake Forest
Michael Travers, editor

Contains sixteen scholarly presentations from the international C. S. Lewis convention in Wake Forest, NC. Walter Hooper shares his important essay "Editing C. S. Lewis," a chronicle of publishing decisions after Lewis' death in 1963. Other contributors include James Como and Sanford Schwartz.

"Scholars from a variety of disciplines address a wide range of issues. The happy result is a fresh and expansive view of an author who well deserves this kind of thoughtful attention." Diana Pavlac Glyer, author of *The Company They Keep: C. S. Lewis and J.R.R. Tolkien as Writers in Community.*

Why I Believe in Narnia:
33 Essays & Reviews on the Life & Work of C. S. Lewis
By James Como

Chapters range from reviews of critical books, documentaries and movies to evaluations of Lewis' books to biographical analysis. In addition to close-up looks, Como reflects on the "big picture" of the most important contributions Lewis has made, not just in literature, but as a social philosopher and reformer. An invaluable tool for appreciating the breadth and depth of Lewis' thinking.

"A valuable, wide-ranging collection of essays by one of the best informed and most astute commentators on Lewis' work and ideas." Peter Schakel, author *Imagination & the Arts in C. S. Lewis*

C. S. Lewis & Philosophy as a Way of Life:
A Comprehensive Examination of his Philosophical Thoughts
By Adam Barkman

C. S. Lewis, renowned Christian apologist and beloved author of children's novels, is rarely thought of as a "philosopher" per se despite having both studied and taught philosophy for several years at Oxford. Moreover, Lewis's long journey to Christianity was essentially philosophical – passing through seven diffeent stages. Barkman incorporate previously unexplored treasures from Lewis's unpublished philoposphy lecture notes, lost philosophical books, such as Aristotle's *Ethics* and Augustine's *City of God* to help chronicle his journey. This 624 page book is an invaluable reference for C.S. Lewis scholars and fans alike.

Harry Potter

Harry Potter & Imagination:
The Way Between Two Worlds
Travis Prinzi

"What we achieve inwardly will change outer reality." Those words, written by Plutarch and quoted by J.K. Rowling her 2008 Harvard commencement speech, sum up both the importance of the *Harry Potter* series and the argument of Travis Prinzi's analysis of the best-selling books in *Harry Potter & Imagination: The Way Between Two Worlds.* Imaginative literature places a reader between two worlds: the story world and the world of daily life, and challenges this reader to imagine and to act for a better world. Starting with discussion of Harry Potter's more important themes, *Harry Potter & Imagination* takes readers on a journey through the transformative power of those themes for both the individual and for culture by placing Rowling's series in its literary, historical, and cultural contexts.

Deathly Hallows Lectures
John Granger

In *The Deathly Hallows Lectures*, John Granger reveals the finale's brilliant details, themes and meanings. Even the most ardent of *Harry Potter* fans will be surprised by and delighted with the Granger's explanations of the three dimensions of meaning in *Deathly Hallows*. Ms. Rowling has said that alchemy sets the "parameters of magic" in the series; after reading the chapter-length explanation of *Deathly Hallows* as the final stage of the alchemical Great Work, the serious reader will understand how important literary alchemy is in understanding Rowling's artistry and accomplishment.

Repotting Harry Potter:
A Professor's Book-by-Book Guide for the Serious Re-Reader
James Thomas

A professor of literature for over thirty years, Dr. James W. Thomas takes us on a tour through the *Potter* books in order to enjoy them in different ways upon subsequent readings. Re-readers will be pleasantly surprised at what they may have missed in the books and at what secrets Rowling has hidden for us to uncover as we revisit these stories. The professor's informal discussions focus on puns, humor, foreshadowing, literary allusions, narrative techniques, and other aspects of the *Potter* books that are hard-to-see on the hurried first or fifth reading. Dr. Thomas's light touch proves that a "serious" reading of literature can be fun.

George MacDonald

Diary of an Old Soul & The White Page Poems
George MacDonald and Betty Aberlin

In 1880, George MacDonald, the Scottish poet, novelist and preacher, published *A Book of Strife in the Form of the Diary of an Old Soul*. The first edition of this book of daily poems included a blank page opposite each page of poems. Readers were invited to write their own reflections on the "white page." MacDonald wrote: "Let your white page be ground, my print be seed, growing to golden ears, that faith and hope may feed." Betty Aberlin responded to MacDonald's invitation with daily poems of her own.

Betty Aberlin's close readings of George MacDonald's verses and her thoughtful responses to them speak clearly of her poetic gifts and spiritual intelligence. Luci Shaw, poet

George MacDonald: Literary Heritage and Heirs
Roderick McGillis

It has been 15 years since Roderick McGillis edited *For the Childlike*, a landmark collection of essays about George MacDonald's writings. This latest collection of 14 essays sets a new standard that will influence MacDonald studies for many more years. George MacDonald experts are increasingly evaluating his entire corpus within the nineteenth century context. This volume provides further evidence that MacDonald will eventually emerge from the restrictive and somewhat misleading reputation of being C. S. Lewis' spiritual "master."

This comprehensive collection represents the best of contemporary scholarship on George MacDonald. Rolland Hein, author of *George MacDonald: Victorian Mythmaker.*

Breinigsville, PA USA
29 September 2009
224955BV00001B/78/P

9 780982 238530